To: JASMIN
MAY EVERY
ALL THE

It's Time To
Recharge

How to Elevate Your Mindset and Increase Your Sales and Business Opportunities

Wayne M. Kuhn

It's Time To Recharge: How to Elevate your Mindset and increase your Sales and Business Opportunities

ISBN: 978-1-77277-376-7

Limits of Liability and Disclaimer of Warranty
The author and publisher shall not be liable for your misuse of the enclosed material. This book is strictly for informational and educational purposes only.

Warning – Disclaimer
The purpose of this book is to educate and entertain. The author and/or publisher do not guarantee that anyone following these techniques, suggestions, tips, ideas, or strategies will become successful. The author and/or publisher shall have neither liability nor responsibility to anyone with respect to any loss or damage caused, or alleged to be caused, directly or indirectly by the information contained in this book.

Published By:
10-10-10 Publishing
Markham, Ontario

First 10-10-10 Publishing in Paperback edition June 2020

Table of Contents

I dedicate this book
to my wife and best friend,
Suzanne Saunders,
whose patience, love and support
are continuous.

Foreword

Have you ever wondered why there are some people who live a happier, more fulfilled life than you? They excel at what they do and live a life of ABUNDANCE, while you live an average existence and just get by.

Would you like to wake up early every morning, jump out of bed, and be excited about your new day ahead?

Would you like to be *Recharged* and feel purposeful every day? Would you like to have an elevated mindset that will attract stronger, more authentic relationships, leading you to higher income?

In his book, *It's Time to Recharge,* Wayne M. Kuhn asks the profound question:

"What do YOU really want?"

If you are a salesperson, entrepreneur, business owner or self-employed person, then I strongly recommend you read this book. It is full of insights, stories and personal examples that will act as a guide in your life of *Recharge* and self-awareness.

If you wonder why the "other guy" is always ahead of you no matter how hard you try, I believe this book will change your life.

If you are stuck, feeling that you are coasting, and need that boost, that reboot, that recharge, then I know this powerful book will *Recharge* you.

Wayne explores with you the gap between where you are today and where you dream of being in the future. Although your knowledge and skills are important, they are not the most important aspect of you becoming successful. You will find out what is in your gap.

I love the way Wayne has taken his life events; simple, easy to follow examples, and stories from his own life as a real estate broker to demonstrate how the principles of *Recharge* can work for you.

You will relate to the metaphors Wayne uses. "The Kitchen Table" and "The Box" demonstrate how you created a paradigm that directs your journey in life. Through elevating your mindset, acknowledgement and awareness, you can shift your paradigm. The new thoughts you have will help you change your actions, generating your desired outcome.

It's Time to Recharge is the book for you. Get ready to create a massive change in your life and begin a new journey toward what YOU really want.

Raymond Aaron
New York Times Bestselling Author

Acknowledgements

As I look around, there are countless people who have contributed to who I am today and to the creation of this book. If I do not mention your name in this acknowledgement, it is not because I appreciate you less, but only that I have limited space.

I begin by acknowledging with great thanks, my parents, Milton and Marjorie. Even though my dad has passed and will not see this book in its completion, I know he is with me always. Thank you, Mom and Dad, for giving me a foundation of faith, love and forgiveness that influenced me to be who I am today.

To my wife, Suzanne Saunders. I am grateful for your continual love, support and understanding through this process. You allowed me personal time and freedom within our relationship. We spent hours of creating and sharing literary ideas together that flowed while writing.

To my family, my brother Brian and my sister Colleen, I express my deepest and most sincere thank you. Also, our sons, Robert, Steven, Scott, Mike, Jay and extended family, thank you. Even though we are all on our individual growth journeys, you were always there to support and encourage me.

To my colleagues at the Black Walnut Toastmaster Club #3320, I thank you for helping me build and practise my communication and leadership skills every week for the past 27 years.

To Bud Brown, DTM, (Distinguished Toastmaster), my Toastmaster mentor and friend. Thank you for believing in me before I believed in myself, and for nudging me forward when I wanted to quit.

To my many friends and colleagues in my office at Re/max Real Estate Centre Inc. and the many others within the Real Estate Industry, I say thank you. Thank you for the past 33 years of fun and challenges along this journey. You shared with me your knowledge and skills as we worked together building our future.

To Louise Stephens, the best Broker/Manager in Re/max, I say thank you. Thank you for all you do for me. You were my cheerleader, encouraged and counselled me, and gave me opportunities to share my *Recharge* message within Re/max.

To my good friend Joe Groh for your long-lasting friendship. You were always there to be my sounding board and to encourage me to dream big. You were the catalyst I needed to step out, be bold and try new things.

To Jacquelyn Mackenzie, leading consultant within the Bob Proctor Institute. Thank you for introducing me to the Proctor Gallagher Institute and their Thinking into Results Leadership program. You opened the door for me, to a new life and a new way of thinking.

To Rev. Dr. Don Moore, my long-time friend and coach. Thank you for your continual support and encouragement. Your wisdom and understanding gave me a new perspective along my journey.

To Gary Jones, a long-time friend that challenged me to think clearly, be specific, have a plan and follow my dream. Thank you for being gentle and understanding. Thank you for being tenacious and persistent, always looking for ways I can do better.

To Janet M. Benedict, Founder of "The Canadian Networker," I say thank you for your support and encouragement. You gave me many opportunities to speak and share *Recharge* with various networking groups and coached me to be the optimistic entrepreneur I am today.

To Raymond Aaron and his 10-10-10 Publishing Program that gave me the structure, guidance and accountability to make this book a reality. Thank you, it's your dream that made my dream a reality. Your energy and enthusiasm are contagious.

And finally, to my many friends, acquaintances and associates I met through my church, networking opportunities, speaking conferences, workshop training, and seminar events that cheered me on and encouraged me to write this book. Here it is. Thank you.

Chapter One

The Birth of Recharge

Why Some People Excel and Others Don't

This could have been the title of this book but instead I chose *It's Time To Recharge.*

If I did answer this question in one sentence, I would likely say, "because we are all different."

There are billions of people in the world and we are all different. Not just in the obvious sense of race and religion, but how we were raised and who was in our space at the most influential time of our life; around the kitchen table.

In the chapters ahead I will touch on many of these areas and find the common thread that weaves through all of us so we can tap into it. This will help create your *Recharge* mindset.

We will explore and acknowledge many things around us that we cannot change and embrace the things we can change, even though at this point you may think that they are fixed attributes. We often have habits that create the same results, and make us feel stuck, unable to see alternatives.

Being stuck is like being on a treadmill, that we are on every day and goes nowhere. We are doing the same things, taking the same actions, getting the same results and wondering why.

Is this you? It is important to stop and become aware of your treadmill, the habits and activities that we do every day; however, there is something very important that goes with awareness. Once you become aware, the change will only happen when you decide what you want: what you *really* want. Only then will the actions you take lead you in the direction of that "want."

Most people are comfortable being stuck. By this I mean that it is easier to stay where they are than to stop what they are doing and do something different.

Change is uncomfortable, disruptive, creates the *what if* fear factor. What if I fail? What if they laugh at me? What if it doesn't work?

Change requires effort; however, staying where you are takes effort as well, but with fewer results.

You will find that Recharge will elevate your thinking, and your mindset, to a higher more productive level and you will find a new you, a new paradigm that will open new doors and create new opportunities.

Your paradigm is the way you look at something. It is your standard, your perspective, your set of ideas. A paradigm is a person's frame of reference. The paradigm is how you see the world based on all the information that you have gathered and the beliefs that you possess.

You may feel uncomfortable at first as you introduce new actions; however, the results you see will convince you that the new Recharged you was well worth it.

The Story of the Red Balloon

You will see red balloons travel with me wherever I go. They are on the cover of this book, on my business cards and promotional materials. I carry a red balloon in my pocket, wherever I go. I thought it necessary to share with you the why, as it has become a big part in recharging me and reminding me to celebrate life and bring joy to others.

My grandson Aidan is now 11 years old. He doesn't have the passion and excitement he used to have when he opens his birthday card and sees that Grandpa Wayne has once again sent him a red balloon.

Let me go back to the beginning. My son Steve came to me one day about 11 years ago and announced that he had just been accepted for a position in the finance department with the Federal Government. I was so proud and happy for him as he worked hard and he deserved this promotion more than anyone I knew.

But wait! They were moving to Ottawa!

Aidan, our first grandson, had been born just six months prior and we were so excited about seeing him grow and be a part of our lives. My first thought was *you can't do this*. A child needs a grandpa. A grandpa needs a grandson.

What would I do? They were moving 6 hours away. It may as well have been to the other side of the world. How would I build a relationship with Aidan? How would I make sure he knows his Grandpa Wayne?

I have always loved red balloons. They remind me to celebrate life and be thankful for what we have. Kids like balloons. Why not send Aidan a birthday card with a red balloon inside?

I thought it would be fun, so whenever I had a chance, Christmas, Easter, birthday, Valentine's Day and every other possible opportunity, I would send Aidan a card and in it I would put a red balloon.

One day I got a call from Laura, Aidan's mom. She mentioned

in conversation that they received the card I had sent for Aidan. She said as they opened it for him the red balloon fell out and onto the floor. Aidan's eyes grew big and she could feel his excitement as he yelled at the top of his lungs, "GRANDPA WAYNE!!!" Keep in mind that Aidan was too young to read and could barely speak in full sentences.

As she told me this, tears came to my eyes for I knew I had achieved my goal. Aidan would remember who Grandpa Wayne is forever.

I still get tears in my eyes just telling you this as it was a major emotional moment for me.

The red balloons are still a big part of my world. You may call it a brand; for me it's a reminder of joy. A reminder to celebrate each moment you can in life. To smile, laugh and be grateful.

If you are a Realtor reading this book you know that we help people go through a stressful event in their lives. If we can reduce that stress and make their move less stressful, even a fun experience, then our job is much easier and they will tell their friends and soon the word will spread.

Fully Charged

Are you 100% fully charged? What does that mean?

It was a typical afternoon at the real estate office. I was sitting in my office in front of my laptop with mouse in hand doing the typical real estate sales person thing, searching for properties for my buyers, going through my leads wondering who I should call first, if any. I remember feeling a bit in a rut. Waiting for the day to end. Ready to go home even though it was mid afternoon. Thinking it was almost coffee time and who could I recruit to commiserate about the last sale I didn't get or the client that isn't answering the email?

As I moved the curser around on the screen it hovered down to the bottom right hand corner, over the battery symbol, and a small window flashed on the screen that said, "FULLY CHARGED!"

It stopped me in my tracks.

Now I knew it meant that the battery on my laptop was 100% fully charged; however, it made me think, am I fully charged? Am I ready to go, working at my maximum? Am I fully charged and what does that mean? How do I get there? Do I need to be Recharged?

When I google the word charged, the references it makes are to electricity or energy but also to great excitement and strong emotions.

This triggered a number of thoughts that ended up with these questions. When was the last time I felt great excitement and strong emotions? Am I excited, energized and fully charged right now? Why not? How do I get to that state, NOW!!?

As a salesperson and self-employed entrepreneur, I knew I had to be fully charged all the time. To be excited and motivated when meeting my clients.

"It's Time to Recharge" was born.

I wrote this book to answer these questions. How do I Recharge, be excited and energized about what I do now, and all the time?

In this book, you will see the correlation between being fully charged, creating better relationships and generating higher income. You will realize how when you are recharged you engage with people at a higher, more personal level. With an elevated mindset you create an unforgettable experience.

The Peter Story

Have you ever wondered why some people excel in life, build large corporations, are top sales people in the office, or manage successful teams generating massive income? Some meet high athletic achievements, climb mountains, win awards and are top achievers with top grades in their class, while others just get by.

Others struggle to pay the bills every month, have jobs that earn minimum wage, drive old cars and live mediocre lives.

Are some people super human beings, gifted above others?

I wrote this book with the intention of answering this question and shedding light on the WHY.

It's easy to look at someone else's accomplishments and achievements and dismiss their wins as being super human, gifted, or if we are really stumped, we may call them lucky.

I recall being in grade school. An old red brick building, built in 1911. At that time, it was built with two classrooms; however, by the time I arrived there were two additional classrooms. Each room had two grades; a bit different than today's classes.

Peter was my classmate and best friend. We played ball, went for bike rides and attended each other's birthday parties. We grew up going to this school together from grade one to grade eight.

Academically I was an average student. I struggled with reading, spelling and some math. I think art was my favourite. Each test was a chore to prepare for. Mom would help as she could by writing down quiz questions on the black board in the kitchen to help me memorize the answers with the goal of getting a passing grade. As I remember, school and learning were stressful.

On the other hand, my friend Peter would leave for home after school empty-handed, and didn't seem to worry about studying. He was a first-class reader and could out spell anyone in the class. He was so smart yet never studied. I thought God made him smart. We would call him gifted. I envied Peter and wished I could get good grades like he did.

As often happens after grade eight we moved away and we ended up going to different high schools (secondary schools). As years passed by, we lost touch with each other.

Forty-three years later I happened to be reminiscing with a cousin of mine who I found out through conversation was friends with Peter's brother. I asked her if she ever crossed paths with Peter. She did. She told me that Peter had just retired. After finishing high school, he went to work for a local construction company delivering wood products to many of the construction sites in the area.

I was dumbfounded. Speechless. Don't get me wrong, there is nothing wrong with what Peter did. You see, I just assumed that after high school he went on to university and then on to be a professional engineer or go on to college and university to be a doctor in some advanced field of Science or medicine or at minimum the CEO of a large cooperation.

Peter had natural talent which would have opened doors to great things. Why didn't that happen? What happened?

Knowing is Not Doing

I come from a place in history where we were told "get a good education and you will go far in life." There are likely many of us that still believe this statement is true, and for the most part it holds water.

If you want to be a professional or researcher in a field, a doctor, lawyer or engineer, then a formal education is a must. The more you focus on a specialized area, the more education you require.

I understand from many youths that making a career choice is not an easy decision. It comes at a time when youth are trying to learn about themselves, what they like and dislike, let alone decide what they want to be when they grow up.

I don't have to look too far to find that many youths attend years of schooling, graduate and never enter the field in which they studied. One may argue this was a waste of time and energy; however, it can be viewed as all part of the educational process and maturing.

Recharging works best when one enjoys what they do and is passionate about the outcome of the activity, whether it be providing a service or a product.

The big WHY pops up again on this page when we see well educated individuals come out of school and not doing anything with that knowledge.

Remember the Peter story? Peter had the talent and ability to learn but something was missing. It was that piece that inspires and motivates an individual to take the knowledge and skill, and reach amazing levels of success.

There is a gap between knowing — having the knowledge and skill to accomplish — and then doing — where we actually take action and do the work.

Recharge will fill that gap between where you are today and where you dream of being in the future.

It's in that gap that we carry the mindset that will determine our level of success. The higher we can elevate our mindset, the more doors of opportunity we can open.

When I passed my real estate exam there were 28 students. We were all taught the same skills and gained the same knowledge we needed to become successful real estate sales people, but today only 3 of us from that class remain in the business. Why? Why were some of us more successful than others?

The answer is in the gap.

Natural Talent vs. Persistence

I built the Recharge program over the past five years with no intention of ever writing a book or putting it into a book form.

My passion is speaking. I am best in front of a group, facilitating a Recharge workshop or speaking on stage in front of an audience, large or small, about Recharge.

I still have a dream to travel the world speaking to thousands of people about Recharge, elevating their mindset to think and function at a higher, more productive level, creating better relationships and generating massive income.

I hope that someday you will take my workshop and personally dive deeper into Recharge.

The book idea came from a need to reach out to more people with the message of Recharge. Writing was not a natural thing for me to do. I came from a back ground where academic skills were average and learning a trade was much more practical and served a useful purpose.

I graduated from a community college with a certificate in Electronics. This had to be the farthest thing from speaking or writing I could be.

We all have a journey and sometimes the path we start out on is not the path we stay on. I have encountered many people with natural talent and skills, who have let them go to waste, spending fruitless time in areas of meaningless toil.

We need only to observe some of the great athletes, politicians and world leaders to see examples of how individuals coming from backgrounds of misfortune have worked hard, persisting until they reach great heights, great success.

You will learn in this book that Recharged people have the mindset of greatness. That it wasn't always about natural ability. There was persistence. A goal, a dream, a vision that catapulted them ahead to victory.

Where are you in your journey? Have you a gap to explore? It's time to RECHARGE.

Discovery Questions:

1/ If you had enough money to live the rest of your life with no worries, what would you be doing right now?

____
____
____
____
____
____
____

2/ What are you passionate about doing? Something you enjoy and feel fulfilled when you do it?

____
____
____
____
____
____
____

The Recharge Model

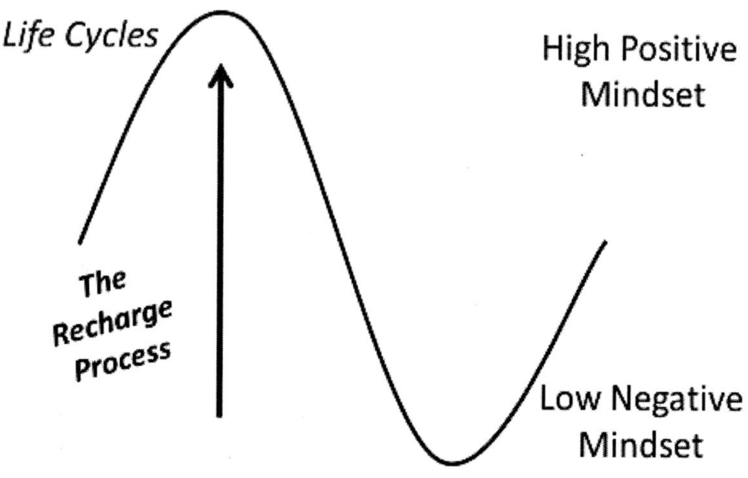

The Recharge Process will raise your mindset to think and function at a higher more positive, productive level, creating powerful, authentic relationships and generating massive income.

Chapter Two

Acknowledge That Life Cycles

Acknowledge and Accept

To acknowledge something is to accept or admit the existence of its truth. We acknowledge that every day the sun goes down in the west and in the morning the sun rises again in the east whether the sky is clear or cloudy.

Gravity is sometimes used as a simple example of a law that, even though we take it for granted, is always there and very necessary. Science has derived ways to overcome the law of gravity and has reached out into space travel to experience the weightlessness of no gravity; however, coming back to earth, gravity is a constant force necessary to hold things in place.

Look at your cup of coffee on the table in front of you. Without gravity the cup would float off the table and suspend in the air. Without gravity the coffee would rise from inside the cup and float into the air. These are the simplest things around us that we take for granted every day.

When you embrace Recharge, there are many things to account for and acknowledge that will help you understand where you are today in life, and why you are where you are.

We look at the five senses that we acknowledge as part of the external input to our thinking and unless we have lost or were born without one of these senses, we acknowledge the ability to see, to touch, to smell, to hear and to taste.

This is an important first step to Recharge. It gives us an opportunity to take inventory and acknowledge the many pieces to the puzzle of our life.

Because we are all different, what we acknowledge from one person to another can be different. We mentioned earlier how some people are born with gifts, where others need to work hard to achieve. Where one person is good at mathematics, another may be good at reading and literature.

Our physical differences may change what we do and how we do things. I am a good example, being six foot in height and weighing around 190 lbs. I may not be a good candidate to be a jockey. Oh, I can ride a horse, but may never win a race as I am too heavy for the horse to achieve any competitive speed.

I will talk about this again; however, it is a good time to mention that a good part of acknowledging is the separation of the fixed vs. the variable. What can we change and what can't we change, and how can we know the difference between the two?

Further on in the book you will find out that there may be, with the right mindset, things you can change that, right now, you feel you can't.

Life Cycles

Have you ever woken up one morning and felt a bit off? Something didn't feel quite right but you couldn't put your finger on it? You try. You start going down your mental list.

Did I go to bed to late? Did I eat something too late or drink too much last night? Was that last coffee too strong? Am I worried about something? The list could be endless . . . so stop it! Shake it off!

I'm sure we have all had these mornings. All I can say is acknowledge that life cycles and so we accept it as normal. Have you ever wondered if you can do something about it?

Someday you may feel more excited about getting up in the morning and living life than other days. Events happen around us that are sometimes out of our control and can have a dramatic effect on how we think and function. Events causing worry and stress that continually occupy our thoughts.

Picture a sine wave with peaks and valleys, highs and lows. Like the tide of the ocean makes the water rise and fall, or the rising and setting of the sun, so too life cycles.

As a salesperson and entrepreneur, I found the cycle of life dramatically effected how I thought and functioned on a day-to-day basis. It was the highs and lows that seemed to control how I felt, and how I felt determined my actions for that day. You can guess the next step. My results were not what I wanted, and that caused a further downward spiral.

If you can identify with this spiral, then Recharge is for you. Don't feel you are alone. Recharge is all about elevating you into a higher zone so you think and function happier, more productive, and more profitable. I will talk more about the rewards of being fully charged in chapters ahead.

As we learn the process and practises of Recharge you will soon realize that, even though we cannot control the life cycle, we can accept it with a new mindset and use this principle of rise and fall, up and down, to our advantage.

What if every morning you woke up early, felt fully charged and ready to take on the day? The idea of feeling a bit off? . . .

Well, it never existed. It was a thought that came out of the lower zone and now is nowhere to be found.

What if no matter what the cycles of life were doing, you maintained control of how you think and feel?

What if? . . .

The Elevated Mindset

Why is this so important?

Our goal in Recharge is to elevate your mindset so you think and function at a higher, more productive level. Before we explore this area of an elevated mindset, that higher zone, what this means and why this is so important in life, let's first look at the lower zone.

When one is on the low side we are preoccupied with worry, fear, doubt, anxiety over a future negative outcome. This mindset can be the result of thoughts that are created either from the subconscious or conscious. They are sometimes labelled as negative thoughts and can be real or fantasy.

They can stem from events that are in our memory from the past or be the result of events happening in the moment. For example:

- As a salesperson you may have just lost a large sale that you were counting on to meet your sales target for the month end.
- As a parent, say your child has not arrived home from school and you are worried that something bad has happened. This is not normal behaviour and your thoughts start to cause you anxiety.

Whatever the cause, the thoughts of these events pull you down into that lower zone.

When you are in the high elevated mindset or making decisions that move you towards this mindset, your thoughts will be filled with gratitude, hope and understanding. You have thoughts of optimism and look for the good in everything within you and around you.

When you awake in the morning, you visualize, expect and plan to have a great day. You are happy and grateful for what you have and what you are going to have in the future.

Why is this so?

Because this is what you choose. These are the thoughts you have chosen to have right now, in this moment. These are conscious thoughts. You are very aware. They are intentional thoughts.

When you are Recharged with an elevated mindset, the results and rewards will overwhelm you to a state of joy and happiness that will expose new exciting opportunities to you.

Doors will open magically for you. You will attract other like-minded people to you. New collaboration and creativity will unfold.

The higher mindset is a growth mindset. It is open to new ideas and fosters your imagination. The creative space works best in the higher zone where dreams, goals and future ideas flourish.

This is why Recharge is so important in giving you an understanding and a process to elevate you into a space where you can think and function at a more productive level. Building better relationships and exposing yourself to opportunities for building wealth should be your goal.

Exciting! . . . But what gets in our way?

External vs. Internal Challenges

The concept of Recharge may look easy on the surface and sound reasonably simple. By changing our mindset, our thoughts, we can change our state from low to high.

The reality is that there are many factors both internal and external that erode our progress and create challenges in recharging. These will vary from person to person, and every situation is different, making the journey of recharge very individual and personal.

Externally, we are referring to the environment around us. Does your environment support you, or does it distract you from moving ahead? Is your environment in harmony with what you want to achieve, the goals you have set, the dreams you have visualized? If not, that upward climb will be even more challenging.

Look closely at your home, where you live, your place of employment, where you work, the relationships you have with family, friends or colleagues. These all contribute to the way you think, and your thoughts determine your state of mind.

You want to create a space around you that is supportive. People with open minds that encourage you with your dreams and goals. I find that surrounding myself with Recharged people helps me stay fully charged, optimistic, and excited about my journey.

Sometimes we just need to do the best we can. Sometimes things are not perfect and we need to cope with the situation we are in. Maybe we have to attend a family event knowing there will be people there that don't share our views and are non-supportive. Maybe we have a client that pushes our buttons and makes us feel uncomfortable.

We each have different circumstances to work with.

Approaching each one with an open mind, expecting good things to happen, will change the dynamics and create a more favourable outcome.

Internally, you would think we have more control. The distractions are different and often more profound because we can't easily escape from them. Our thoughts are with us wherever we go, and so we must learn to control, reprogram, and create new thought patterns.

Each of us comes from a different place. In the next chapter we will dive deeper into some of the reasons we think the way we do, and look at the different paradigms we all have, but for now let's take this moment of time and examine some of the internal challenges we have.

Having an optimistic mindset is a good start. Starting with thoughts of gratitude will often put you in the high mindset of "I Can." Think about the wins in your life, the times when things went well, when you made that sale you were not sure of, or when you ran that last kilometre of your first 10K run.

These wins will help replace your thoughts of "I can't," that preoccupied your mind with worry, fear and doubt, and created anxiety. It takes practise and effort to maintain a conscious, elevated mindset.

I like to compare our mind, our ability to think, to a muscle. For example, if you were wanting to run a marathon you might join a gym to get in shape. You might change your diet so you eat healthier. You would run every day to practise for the marathon. Each day you run, it would get easier and you would be running further, until the day of the marathon you felt confident you could do this.

Treat your mind the same way. It will take practise and daily effort to program your thoughts to be in harmony with Recharge. Visualizing what you want, setting your goals and making a plan are things you do intentionally. Using your imagination, practising creative thinking and having an open mind all require you to have intentional mindfulness.

You will, after a while, build courage in this place of self-awareness. This courage will develop into self-confidence and build your self-esteem. You will empower yourself and, like the runner in the marathon, you will be ready and know you are fully charged and prepared.

Along the way are many external distractions that will test you. They will give you lower thoughts and thought patterns that erode your positive mental attitude. I leave it up to you to discern whether you can handle these distractions or block them out.

It is my recommendation that it will be easier to Recharge and maintain an elevated mindset in its purist form if you reduce or in most cases eliminate these distractions. You may have guessed, I am referring to the news, violent TV shows, video games, and other sources of communication or information that cause you stress and worry.

Being aware and mindful of your thinking, what affects your thoughts, gives you control of your mindset.

Highs and Lows

In the context of Recharge, I mention two states of mind, a high and a low. High being the top of the cycle, or sine wave, when you are feeling your best, and low being at the bottom of the cycle or sine wave when you are feeling at your worst.

It may sound at this point a bit black and white, meaning you are either high or low. This is not the case. We are never completely one or the other. Rather look at it as something that is dynamic; constantly moving. The movement is either towards the high or towards the low. If you prefer a polarity analysis you are either moving towards the positive or towards the negative.

The movement is not a physical move but a mindset shift. We are thinking either towards the high or towards the low, based on our thoughts in the moment. We never stop thinking so there is no neutral. There is no time when you are not thinking.

Within our thoughts we are constantly making decisions. Choices of thought, what to think, choices of actions and what to do. The thoughts we have and activities we do either move us towards the high or towards the low.

You would think this is obvious; however, we are not always conscious of the decisions we make. Our paradigm causes us to make decisions from our subconscious, our automatic pilot, rather than from a place of being consciously aware all the time. We have developed habits and behaviours that are routine. Some are good and some are not. Some steer us high and some steer us low.

The challenge comes in being mindfully aware of our thoughts and deciding if they are thoughts that elevate us to the high zone rather than decline us to the low zone.

Being aware of our thoughts seems very simple; however, we will learn that even though it may sound simple, many of us are not aware or conscious of our thoughts and so our mind drifts on automatic pilot guided by a paradigm that is destined for sameness.

The objective of Recharge is to educate and give you a process to move from a low mindset to higher mindset. This will change your paradigm by being mindful of what is going on around you, and through this new awareness you will develop a new higher-level of habits and behaviours that will elevate your thinking.

What is required to do this? What will it take? Why is this important?

If these are your questions, then Recharge is for you.

Let's explore this higher level.

Your Strengths and Weaknesses

If you recall, in the first chapter, the story of Peter, and how even though he had inherent natural abilities to learn and was strong academically, one may conclude he didn't achieve great things in life.

We are all born with some natural ability, an attribute that we seem to excel at with less effort than others. It maybe our physical strength, our height, or our appearance that was a genetic trait passed done through our family history. A nose, a hair line or even a disposition that is envied by others.

The list could be endless but I think you get the point. These are characteristics passed on to us. It is sometimes controversial to suggest that other genetic traits are passed down through our ancestors but sometimes we see attitudes, beliefs and behaviours are passed down as well. We will look closer at these in our next chapter.

Being aware of your characteristics is important to who you are and what you become. Have you noticed that basketball players tend to be very tall? That doesn't say if you are shorter that you can't play basketball. You may just have to work harder at it and overcome some stereotypical beliefs about basketball players and the game.

It is advisable to make a list of these traits. Ask others around you that know you well, what they observe to be your strengths.

Once you have a good knowledge of your strengths you can use these attributes to spring board into a career, profession or occupation where you can best use them.

In Recharge we teach and encourage you to celebrate your natural gifts. Too many times we take these for granted, downplay these gifts in modesty and overlook our great potential. People look at us in envy as we squander away our natural talent that could open doors of opportunity for us. The list will empower us to be aware of who we are and what we can achieve.

When I was in grade school I never liked to read. My challenge was that I would read a story then as part of the exercise had to answer questions about what I read. I could never remember what I read so consequently I couldn't answer any of the questions. I am guessing that my dislike for reading also affected my spelling as I would fail at it as well. I went through college and on to university never reading a book completely from cover to cover, and relied on Cole's Notes to give me a passing grade.

I share this with you because this was a weakness of mine. At the time I was embarrassed about it but compensated the best I could. Looking back now, with the proper guidance and instruction I could have overcome this weakness much earlier in life. Today, I am a much stronger reader and I love books.

We all have weaknesses; things we are not strong at and don't do well at. Many of them can be overcome through Recharge with a shift in our paradigm. Sometimes it is a fear or belief that is holding us back.

In the business world we encourage you to reach out to other professionals with expertise you may not have. Hire an accountant to organize your books. A painter to paint your office. A plumber to fix the sink.

Identifying your strengths and weaknesses is important for your journey to Recharge.

Discovery Questions:

1/ Think of a time when you had to make a major decision. A career change or a move. Did you think towards a higher mindset, all the good reasons or a lower mindset, all the reasons not to?

____
____
____
____
____
____
____

2/ What are some internal and external challenges you have in maintaining a higher, positive mindset? What are some routines, habits or daily activities you could change to affect the outcome?

____
____
____
____
____
____
____

Chapter Three

The Kitchen Table

In The Beginning

We all come from different backgrounds, childhoods or family units. Some we are very proud of, blessed to be a part of, and others we are indifferent to. Some are abusive, destructive, controlling, limiting, while others offered hope, encouragement and support.

This is what makes us all individuals, unique and different. This was one of the challenges in creating Recharge. To find that one thing, the common thread, that is the same amongst everyone. You may call it the thread that binds.

As I reflect back on my roots, my upbringing, the foundation of who I am, I remember the kitchen table and how it played an important part in my beginnings. Not from a perspective of what was on the kitchen table, but who sat at the table with me in my early years.

I realized that at the kitchen table, from the discussions and conversations that were had, I developed my values, my beliefs and my habits, many of which are still embedded deep in the fibre of my character. Here is where my first paradigm was formed.

I was raised on a 100-acre farm, a few miles from a small village in Waterloo County. It was a mixed farm in that we didn't specialize in one thing but had a mixture of crops and animals. I lived there from the time I was 2 years old until the age of 14, when we sold the farm and moved to the big city.

I remember that time very well. My dad, who has since passed away, said he sold the farm because farming was getting more complicated with new regulations of what you can grow and what products you can produce.

The sale of the farm in 1967 was very lucrative and laid a strong financial foundation for my dad and his family.

No debt and money in the bank.

Family

I have a brother who is 3 years older than me and a sister who is 9 years younger than me.

I like to joke that I was an only child, but they may argue this point. For many years I was the only child at the kitchen table with my mom and dad. This was prior to my sister being born and my brother going off to school and then to work. My brother and I seemed to be on separate paths, although occasionally the paths would cross with not a lot in common. He was at that stage where he loved cars and girls, and I had little to no interest in either.

It was a time in history when the parental roles were more clearly defined.

My dad would work long hours in the barn, tending to the animals. He was up early in the morning and sometimes worked late into the evening. During the day he was on the fields working the land, planting crops and then harvesting. That was the cycle of farming. He took great pride in what he did and always wanted to do the right thing. He developed a personal relationship with the animals and loved to sing to them.

My mom would tend to the chores and family in and around the house. Cleaning, cooking and making sure the meals were ready at meal time. She was the taxi for us, taking us to school and other events kids go to. Occasionally the lines of responsibility would cross between mom and dad, but generally there was a clear division and distribution of roles and responsibilities.

Both had strong work ethics and believed that making progress and being successful were the result of working hard and saving money. True or false, these two beliefs are still engrained in my paradigm.

Being raised in a Mennonite community of Christian faith we lived a more conservative lifestyle where we had what we needed and were always thankful for what we had. The desire to have financial wealth, travel the world and achieve great things was suppressed by a humble attitude of gratitude. A passive approach to life was prevalent. Seldom challenging the status quo, avoiding conflict at any cost.

Attending church every Sunday was part of our routine as regular as getting up in the morning. These beliefs and attitudes also became who I am and were engrained in me.

The list of values, beliefs and habits that I inherited are likely endless. You can see the power of the kitchen table, and how just sitting at it day after day, and hearing the discussions and conversations that my parents had, influences who I am today.

Being Average

This was me. I had a great childhood with loving parents.

There was always lots to do on the farm. I had cousins that

would come and visit, and we loved to play together. We would explore in and around the barn like pirates or hunters to see what adventures were ahead. I remember digging a hole in the sand box, wondering how far it was to get to China. Someone told me it was on the other side of the world.

At this kitchen table I developed the attitude I have about money. That you should save it and never buy what you can't afford. That debt was bad and should be paid off as soon as possible.

I learned to forgive first and be responsible. To say I'm sorry, and make things right.

I always viewed myself as average. We had all we needed and if we wanted for more that was silly, dumb, maybe even wrong. Maybe even selfish and greedy.

I remember asking the question, are rich people bad and evil? Were they always aggressive and rude? Were they dishonest and did they like to cheat others?

I remember the time Sam, a man we knew from church, came to church driving a big fancy new red car and I wondered why he wouldn't buy a smaller car and give some of that money to the poor.

These were a few of the many thoughts and beliefs I carried with me.

As you reflect back on your own life and your kitchen table you may realize that your situation was more complicated. That you were not always at the same table or the people at the table you were at kept changing, and it was confusing.

It's time to acknowledge that as a child, wherever you were or whatever circumstances you were in, was not your choice. As a child you didn't have a choice as to what kitchen table you sat at or even who was at the table with you.

You were just there, like an innocent, vulnerable sponge,

open and accepting of every value, habit and belief, good or bad, and you believed it all as truth. It became who you are. It is the foundation of you, me, us.

STOP!

Fast forward to today. Here and now. We are mindful in the present. You are sitting at the kitchen table. Is it the same table as you were at as a child? For most of us the answer is no (unless you are like me and inherited many of our parents' hand-me-downs).

Who is at your kitchen table with you today?

This may be a new realization for many of us, but we are no longer that child. In some cases, we are the parent, grandparent, guardian, councillor, friend or relative.

We are no longer at the table because that is where we ended up. We are at this table because of the choices we have made in life. We chose to sit here at this table with these people.

Another profound reality. The habits, beliefs and values we learned and absorbed at the kitchen table as children . . . we brought with us to our new table.

As we talk more about the Recharge process, I will share more. Even though I remember my childhood as a fun and pleasant experience, there were things that I was taught that held me back. In the next chapter we will look in that box.

Mom Today

My mom is 92 and as of now in great health with total independence. She even drives her own car. She is very active and has many friends that are close, and they include her in many activities and social functions. I attribute her long life to her living a life of gratitude.

She doesn't travel the world, but goes to church every week.

I think she is happy, although when I ask her, she doesn't always know what to say because it was never a question asked of her. I love her dearly and she is one of my best friends. I try to visit with her once a week so I can hear her tell stories from the past as I know she will not be here forever.

My mom is still thrifty, and saves money as that is what she knows. I found this out when my dad passed away. She called me and wondered if I would help her manage her financing. I met with her at her apartment and she brought out all the paperwork from the banks and credit union. As she reviewed the accounts with me, I noticed her chequing account. Her balance was $47,481.00. I looked again as I thought it might be her savings account. No, it was the chequing account.

I asked her why she had such a large balance in her chequing account as I knew the interest rate was next to nothing. She didn't think it was that large. Her reply was, "Well, you never know when you might need it." I surmised that this was a comfort factor for her. Something that gave her security.

I went home that day chuckling to myself about Mom's chequing account. I was able to convince her to put half of it into her savings account to get a higher interest rate.

A few days later, I was sitting at my computer paying some bills when the "kitchen table" stared me in the face. I too had a large balance in my chequing account! Why? It is what I was taught at the kitchen table as a child.

I share this with you because you, like me, will not Recharge without being aware of what you learned at your kitchen table when you were a child.

Take the good that you learned and bring it to your present kitchen table. Leave behind the values and beliefs that are not in line with who you want to be. **You decide!**

Today is a new Day!

News Flash!!!

We are now adults and get to choose which kitchen table we sit at. Who is at the table with us now? We can also change and move to another table, should we choose to do so. Start a new table or join someone else's table.

I decide and you decide.

As a child we didn't have that option to choose. As an adult we do.

In saying this, many times we are stuck at a kitchen table that we don't want to be at but don't have the courage, the will or desire to move due to fear of change, obligation or guilt.

I understand and empathize with you that we have responsibilities that we cannot abandon. As a recharged person you will be aware of your own paradigm, and now you can choose what happens at your table. You can take the lead, elevate the level of mindset and conversation happening at the table.

As a salesperson you can ensure that you come to your clients table fully charged and ready to give them your best. An experience they will remember and share with others.

When you are ready to recharge, reach out to embrace a higher mindset, you will be faced with the values, habits and beliefs that you learned as a child at the kitchen table. We like to think that our roots, the teachings from our childhood, were all conducive to a life worth living. A life of encouragement and praise so that we are able to enter the world armed with the tools we need to build massive empires, huge skyscrapers, great families and healthy communities.

Unfortunately, many and most of us didn't have that experience.

Now we can choose. My parents taught me to be grateful, to be thrifty and thankful for what I have. I keep those values today; however, I add in new values and beliefs as well.

I look at opportunities to grow and learn. I look for open doors that I can walk through and take on new adventures. I learn to invest in my future. I look at money as something to spend and invest rather than to accumulate.

Discovery Questions:

1/ Take some time and recall what the kitchen table was like when you were a child. Who was at the table? What did they talk about? Was it an encouraging environment for you?

2/ Make a list of five habits or beliefs you have that you think may have come from your childhood kitchen table. Are they serving you or is it time to make some changes?

Chapter Four

The Box

Picture Your Mind

Put the book down and close your eyes.

I want you to visualize your mind. What picture or image do you see? Do you see a brain, a ball of pink and blue tubes and wires all in a cluster, a light bulb, or some biological formation that you recall seeing in a *National Geographic* magazine? Maybe a smoky, haze-filled room, quiet and dreary. What is it you see?

You may open your eyes now.

I found this exercise very challenging.

There is no right or wrong answer. It is like asking you to picture energy or oxygen. We see the effects of what it does but the thing itself has no shape or physical mater. The term "mental image" is sometimes used as a way of describing the mind or what it creates.

What you pictured with your eyes closed would have been based on memories or images you had stored away. Experiences from the past. Each one of us may have had different images stored away. If we shared with each other what we saw, there may have been some similarities.

I have chosen to equate the mind to a box. If I say to you "picture a box," everyone relates to the image I refer to and your mind immediately sees a box of some form. Now let's say it is a cardboard box, five inches square, wrapped in brown wrapping paper. Printed on the one side of the box are the words "Your mind."

I venture to say that we all have a similar image of this box. Or, at least something close.

P.S. I have this box on my desk in front of me. It helped me with the description. I use it as a prop in my workshops to help people who have challenges visualizing. It makes it real for them.

You can see that even this simple exercise we just did, creating a box, requires our focus on detailed thought and visualization, something we will appreciate more later on in this book as we unwrap our recharge strategy.

Some of you are already jumping ahead of me asking what is in the box. What does it weigh? If you need to, pick it up and shake it. What did you discover? Silly, it's a metaphor.

Now that you know what your mind looks like, let's explore what is inside. It's what is inside that will determine your capacity to Recharge and elevate your mindset.

Inside the Box

What is inside the box?

Let's recall from the previous chapter, "The Kitchen Table." Recall that many of the values, habits and beliefs you hold on to came from the early conversations, teachings and observations you experienced there, at the kitchen table.

These influences were key in forming our mindset early on in life.

They are embedded into our mind and even deeper into our

subconscious mind, meaning we are not always aware of them. They are automatic. They are who we are. They form our paradigm.

For example, remember my mom and her money, and how I was taught as a child to save my money, and now today I still like the feeling of security when I have money in the bank. Especially an excessive, nonlogical, nonsensical amount?

This is programmed in my mind, this is in "My Box."

I remember my first day of school and how I was so anxious that I was too sick to go the first few days.

This is programmed in my mind, this is in "My Box." I am sure you can think of hundreds of memories from as early as you can remember. Memories both good and not so good, moments of sadness and moments of joy and celebration. These are all part of who we are and they are all in "Your Box."

As you get older, go to school, college, university and gain more knowledge, skills, and life experiences, you can see that your box gets filled with many more thoughts, beliefs, ideas and memories. These experiences create our beliefs and habits both good and bad; both right and wrong.

There is an old saying, "Never discuss politics or religion with a stranger." Now you may understand why. Politics or religion tend to be very divisive. Because of the differences of what's in our boxes, these discussions can be very polarized, opinionated and heated unless you come at it with a very open mindset.

When we speak and share our ideas, our opinions, it all comes from our box.

I am not a psychologist or scientist; however, there are studies that show what is in our box may come through the DNA of our ancestors. I cannot comment further on this.

We also acknowledge at this point that each person has their own box. It is unique and different. This is important to accept in the process of recharge as it will be more evident in chapters to come.

I hope you are starting to think about what is in your box. Next, we will have a look outside the box.

Outside the Box

I remember the day I realized that influences can affect my box from the outside.

I was writing in my office, something I love to do. My grandson, Arlan, had just arrived with his parents for a visit. It wasn't long after exploring the house that he found my whereabouts saying "Grandpa Wayne!"

Arlan ran into my office with the confidence of a two-year-old, stopped abruptly, looking around with inquisitive but mischievous eyes. He walked over to my desk. He picked up my box, sized it up, turned around and with all the strength he could muster, threw it across the room with a scream and a laugh.

I have to admit in that moment I had mixed emotions. The whole scene appeared very humorous, for I have to think he may have equated the box to a ball with a new shape.

My second thought came with an "Oh no! My box will be ruined." I had visions of it crashed, dinted and destroyed.

I quickly came off my chair and retrieved my box. With haste I grabbed a red balloon from my drawer and used it to distract this two-year-old intrusion from his new-found object, "My Box."

Outside the box are many distractions. Where we work, live and play all have influence on our mindset. The environment can be a supportive and encouraging place that elevates your mindset to a higher, more productive zone or the environment can be the opposite, taking away your energy and desire to achieve.

It's like you saying to yourself, I have this box, my box, now where do I want to set it?

Many people are not aware of the many influences around them every day. The news we listen to through TV, radio, and now smart phones can be very informative; however, it can also drain our mindset and create lower energy through worry, doubt and uncertainty.

Do the movies you watch, books you read, YouTube you watch and discussions you have with others lift you up, or drag you down?

You may think that one murder mystery will not hurt you once in a while. It's just entertaining, and you're likely right. However, a bit here and there adds up and soon a steady diet of negative can only make you more negative.

When I decided to lose some weight, if I treated myself to a butter tart now and then, maybe once a week, it really didn't affect my overall weight goal that much. However, one leads to two and soon you are having 3-4 butter tarts a week and wondering why you are not losing weight.

A Recharged mind is continually aware of what is influencing the box from the outside. Don't discount anything at this point.

Creating New Habits

My self-awareness increased the more I learned of what was in my box. I could see more clearly who I am, and why I am the way I am. In my case I could see similar traits I have from my mother and father.

It's also interesting to look at my brother and sister and observe what traits they picked up from the kitchen table. Just because we were at the same table doesn't mean we came away with the same box full of goodies. We are all different.

Over the past six years I have worked and studied to explore what is in my box. It is my objective through the writing of this book and sharing my experiences with you, that you too will take inventory of what is in your box. Once you know what is in your box you can see that there are beliefs, values and habits that are not in line with what you want in life, or who you want to become.

I refer back to my kitchen table where building wealth was not a priority as we were thankful for what we had, and had all we needed. This mindset was in conflict with a mindset of abundance, knowing that the more wealth I have, the more I can give away and help those less fortunate than me.

Even though I came from a great loving family and have no regrets, there are habits I brought with me in my box that were not necessarily the best choices.

Creating new habits is necessary to make changes and elevate your mindset to a higher zone where growth, creativity and prosperity dwell.

"What do I really want?" is the question you should be asking yourself on a regular basis. The more times you ask, over time the answer will start to come to you. As you recharge and start to function in the higher mindset you will start to develop a crystal-clear vision of what you want.

Creating new habits will only happen when you know what you want. You will develop a recharge filter that will help you decide what characteristics in your box you want to keep and which ones you want to let go of. This is not always a black and white decision, as some components are obvious and need to be discarded and others are more difficult to identify.

When I was young, I had an uncle that I adored. He was funny, smart, and a successful business man with lots of money. He would bring us gifts and take us for ice cream. The perfect uncle.

As I grew older, I realized my perfect uncle smoked and would occasionally drink too much. I was confused because I couldn't understand how someone so smart and well-liked would do such a harmful thing. Yes, smoking is harmful to your health.

I tell you this because we seldom achieve perfection. There are things we may need to just accept, especially if they are out of our control.

I love to eat. I think there is something in my box that says eat whenever you get a chance. My parents always made me eat everything on my plate. Do you think there is a correlation here?

Challenging the Box

You are likely familiar with the metaphor, "thinking outside the box." What does this mean?

Thinking outside the box is a metaphor that means to think differently, unconventionally, or from a new perspective. This phrase often refers to novel or creative thinking.

The Recharge program is a strong advocate of "thinking outside the box." Creativity is the product of having a higher mindset. Creativity comes from having dreams, visions and goals.

When looking deep into your box, you will see there are often conflicting beliefs. You can see that sometimes you have a thought that has affixed to it a strong belief. Maybe this belief came out of your childhood or from some experience along the way. These are sometimes obvious and sometimes we don't see them until someone else brings them to our attention. Once you acknowledge the belief, and you are aware of its presence, then you can start to make changes to modify, reduce or eliminate it.

We also get stuck on a belief by making it a truth. This is a way of strengthening a belief and giving it deeper roots. Deeper roots mean harder to remove or modify. Religion and politics often fall in this category of deeper roots. Not easily changed, although I am seeing a shift with the younger generation where these roots are not as deep, and change comes easier and more frequently.

We attach truth to the decisions we make all the time. Think about the car you drive. Many people pick a car because it looks nice and stylish, feels and smells good, is fast and the colour is sharp. Sound familiar? Now when we describe it to our friends it is spacious inside, four doors, good warranty and gets great gas mileage. The emotional reason we picked the car is supported by the logical truth we gave it.

If your goal is to be a successful, top producing real estate salesperson, then having a new car may be a good idea. Driving clients around town showing them homes in an old car may be viewed as less than successful. Perception says a new car portrays success, and everyone wants to deal with a successful salesperson to get the best service. Right? Note that this could be another belief straight from the box that may or may not be the truth.

This process is very common and the decisions come from inside your box. If you answered the question," What do I really want?" is the answer a new car? It may be, if this is where you are in life; however, I encourage you to think bigger. Elevate your mindset.

As I sorted through my box, I found some important characteristics I decided to keep as part of who I am. They are traits that you will find in the higher mindset and will serve you well as you search for what you want. They are honesty and integrity.

There is a tendency as we step outside the box to forget the good that is still in the box. The talk of new ideas and buying into new truths may collide with our present paradigm.

When I decided what I want in life, I kept honesty and integrity in my box. I found them on the high side of my mindset. They are part of me. My authentic self.

Closing the Box

We never want to close the box.

We never want to stop adding to the box through growth from education and life experiences. This feeds our creativity, our dreams, our goals.

At the risk of repeating myself, Recharge will elevate your mindset so you think and function at a higher, more productive level.

This higher level is the positive zone, the growth zone we seek. A zone that holds thoughts and feelings of optimism, hope and achievement. A zone that is filled with joy, fun and laughter. A zone where peace, love and contentment are found.

Remember this is a journey, not a destiny. It is a zone we strive to move towards through every decision we make.

The day we close the box is the day we stop growing. A fixed mind is a closed mind.

I hope you have enjoyed the box metaphor of the mind. I hope you will take the time you need to better understand and unpack what is in your box.

Take a look around and observe what is around you. Become aware of things you do and thoughts that you have. Why do you do certain things a certain way? Why are you having the thoughts you are having in this moment? Are they growth thoughts or closed thoughts that are fixed to a certain belief?

As I sit at my laptop, I noticed I have rolled up the sleeves on my shirt, one roll on each sleeve. I can say I do this so my sleeves are out of the way, giving me freedom to type. I can say that I find long sleeves restrictive. The truth may be that I think it looks sharp.

When I see a man conducting a workshop with his jacket off and his sleeves rolled up, I think he means business. Ready to get to work.

What are you doing right now? Why are you doing it?

What we do and think day to day is important to how effectively we Recharge. What we hold in our box is also very important to how effectively we Recharge.

Strategy and techniques on how to manage what's in your box will be explored in chapters ahead.

Discovery Questions:

1/ Start to explore what is in your box. Take an activity, ie: getting dressed in the morning. Make a list of what you do and how you do things. Has it changed over the last year? If so, why did it change?

____

____

____

____

____

____

____

2/ Looking in your box of life experiences, what are some of the major events that are in your box? Have you created a truth around that event? Is there a belief that you need to rethink? ie: Sometimes we react and come to a conclusion too quickly.

____

____

____

____

____

____

____

Chapter Five

Thoughts Create Feelings

State of Mind

I woke up this morning, and headed for the kitchen to start my morning route of Recharge. Something wasn't quite right. Have you ever had a morning where you were feeling a bit off?

I stopped and asked myself, "What am I thinking?"

I had written an offer to purchase on a property the night before, presented it to the seller's agent and was waiting for them to reply back. It was the perfect property for my clients, as they were wanting to downsize from a larger home into this smaller condominium. I was worried we would get turned down and my clients would lose the condo of their dreams. They would be devastated. We had spent many weeks viewing other condominiums and this was the one. I could feel it.

The "what if" thoughts were racing through my head like a speeding freight train, out of control! It was all-consuming. These thoughts of doubt and uncertainty were derailing me from my morning Recharge.

How can I coach others on "how to" when I am feeling so out of control?

What was I thinking?

What if? . . .what if they lose this condo? What will they do? Can I keep them as a client? Will they find another condo that they love just as much as this one?

I was building a story in my mind, filled with worry, failure and disappointment. The more detail I gave it, the more real it became.

This is an example of how we function when we let our thoughts slide to the negative space. To the lower state where we lose touch with reality. We need to stop the slide!

Let's look at the same scenario, only this time we make a shift and think elevated thoughts.

I woke up this morning, headed for the kitchen to start my morning route of Recharge. Something wasn't quite right. I was feeling a bit off.

I stopped and asked myself, "What am I thinking?"

I had written an offer to purchase on a property the night before, presented it to the seller's agent and was waiting for them to reply back. It was the perfect property for my clients, as they were wanting to downsize from a larger home into this smaller condominium.

It is at this point, being aware of what I am thinking, I Recharge, I shift my thoughts to a higher level.

This is a Recharge Moment. We will expand on the Recharge moment in Chapter Seven.

Shift Your Thoughts

Repeat this affirmation three times:

"I am a confident, professional Real Estate Agent. People like and trust me!" X 3

I shifted my thoughts to:

- These are great clients and love working with me.
- They like and trust me and we have fun working together.
- I have done my best and my deals always come together.
- If they lose this condo there will be others.
- I am so grateful these clients picked me to work with.

Can you feel the shift? Are you standing taller? Is there a smile on your face?

This shift, this Recharge, is a small example of what we can do to avoid the start of a downward slide.

We build stories in our conscious thoughts every day. They are often constructed from a base of fear. What if this happens? Some will argue and justify this fear from actual events that happened. They hold on to that memory as a legacy of value and truth. Facts that justify the emotion of fear. Facts that give life to the fear and give it power.

It is a good thing to remember and learn from an event. In most cases fear is a thought that seldom comes true.

The Powerful Mind

Recharge is about making good choices. Decisions that elevate our mindset. We are making decisions as to what thoughts to have at any given moment. Sometimes these thoughts are responsive or intentional, other times they are reactive, totally automatic. Straight from the box.

I recall this phrase from my notes of a seminar I attended many years ago:

"When you get up in the morning you have a choice, you can decide whether you want to have a good day, or a bad day."

Some people may want to argue that life is much more complex than this. That circumstances, events and situations make it such that it is not that simple.

Believe me, it is this simple. It is a choice. It is your choice. You decide! Further on in the book we talk about the perfect morning and how a perfect morning will change the direction of your life.

Your mind is powerful and will determine your destiny, if you use it correctly. By correctly I mean, recharge it regularly through being mindfully aware of your thoughts.

If we remember "The Box," and what is in it, we realize how complex our thinking process is. That our mind is processing information from the past, taking in new information continuously from the present, and then we dream and plan of what our future will be, or could be, and we jam all that in the box.

If you think your mind is busy now, let's throw a problem or a crisis into the mix, and see what it does now.

A busy life filled with responsibility, a family, a career and all the other activities that we are faced with.

STRESS! . . . OVERLOAD! . . . WORRY! . . .

If we were an engine we would be smoking, getting hot and maybe blowing up. Not being an engine, we still sometimes burn out.

I don't discuss burn-out or depression in this book because I am not qualified to do so; however, I think you should be aware of it. It is worth mentioning as it affects Recharging your mindset.

Burn-out is a state of emotional and mental exhaustion caused by excessive stress over time. It occurs when you feel overwhelmed, emotionally drained, and unable to meet constant demands.

Depression is an illness that involves the body, your mood, and your thoughts. It affects the way you eat, sleep, feel about yourself and think about things. Your mindset.

Anyone in a state of burnout or depression should seek professional medical help immediately. If it is unattended it can lead to long-term disastrous results.

It is my opinion, following a process of continually Recharging will assist in long-term mental stability and may help you avoid depression and burnout.

The mind is powerful. In an elevated state, it can attract and create amazing results.

Rest the Mind

"I'm only human, . . . I'm only one person, . . . I can only do so much . . . I'm tired."

These are expressions we often hear when someone is overwhelmed by a task or in a mindset where they feel life is crashing down around them. Their box is full and busy.

My dad taught me respect. Not just to be respectful of other people but to respect our possessions.

I remember whenever he was driving in the rain and came home with the car all wet, he would wipe it down and make sure it was clean and dry before parking it in the garage. He looked after it. He always had regular maintenance done like changing the oil, checking the tires and making sure the gas tank was full for the next excursion.

Dad's cars would last forever. His last one was a 1998 Pontiac. Mom and Dad drove it for 17 years.

We need to respect our body and mind in the same way. We

need to look after them and make sure they are maintained regularly, just like my dad looked after his cars.

Your mind needs to rest.

As each one of us is different you may think that we all rest differently. I would equate it to eating. We may eat different foods but the end result is we all must eat.

We may rest in different ways, but we all need rest. Rest is important to allow us to clear our minds so we can Recharge and think clearly.

My wife and I have a cottage for this exact reason. It allows us to escape the hustle and bustle of life, the busy city and spend some quiet time around the rocks, trees and water. The air is clear and it allows us to clear our thoughts and connect with nature.

You may not have a cottage but may enjoy a vacation away. When you leave your home and enter into a new environment it shifts your thinking away from things that cause you stress and allows your mind to clear and Recharge.

You may choose to go for a walk, in a nearby park to rest. My wife and I love to sit on the park bench and watch the squirrels play. They run and jump and chase each other. We laugh and comment on their behaviour. We soon feel our minds start to clear.

I have many friends that rest in a book. They say, "There is nothing better than sitting back in a comfortable chair with a good book." This is another way of focusing your mind on a story or fantasy helping us escape our own reality in that moment.

There are many ways to rest your mind. Rest is essential for Recharge and long-term mental health.

How do you rest?

Your Role on Stage

Halloween, celebrated October 31st, is always an exciting time of the year. A tradition of dressing up in costumes of all sorts ranging from real-life characters like firefighters or doctors, to characters from fantasy like scary monsters or super heroes. The list is endless.

I remember when our boys were young, they would anticipate the coming of Halloween weeks before the actual day. The discussion would start with, “What do you want to be for Halloween?”

Ideas would be shared until one would say with certainty, “I want to be Spiderman!”

At that point the discussion would continue with why, and would end up with a drive to the store and the purchasing of a Spiderman costume. We had to be careful not to buy it too far in advance or they would want to wear it all the time in anticipation of the big day.

Remembering when we were children and embracing the idea of being a character is something we should revisit.

If we look at life as a stage and we are one of the actors, what role would we play? What character would we be? This was asked of me in a workshop I participated in and I found it a profound question.

Earlier we alluded to the idea that we can control our thoughts, and that creates how we feel. If we take this to the next step, what do we visualize in our thoughts? If you are a Real Estate Broker as I am, what does that look like? What vision is created? Not what is, but what could be? Remember;

Recharge bridges the gap between where you are today and where you dream of being in the future.

At this point in life you may not want to be Spiderman or Wonder Woman; however, you may want to have a close look at the character you are playing and ask yourself, "Is this who I want to be?"

Being mindful of this character you are playing, your role on the stage of life, is an important awareness to have. When you think of this character do you feel good about it? Do you have elevated thoughts of Recharge?

When my son, Robert, said, "I want to be Spiderman!" his eyes lit up and were big and bright. You could feel his energy and excitement as he jumped up and down with great anticipation. He had a vision, an idea and knew what he wanted. He knew what character he wanted to be for Halloween.

Create the leading character you want to be. A leading role on the stage of your life. One that lights up your eyes, gets you excited in anticipation of what the future has in store for you.

I remind you to have an open mind when thinking about this character. Remember there are things in the box, your personal box, that will resist this trajectory. This may be new for you. Like the mind of a child, you are free to use your imagination and create this new character.

We start first in our imagination, then in our thoughts, and then in our feelings.

Building your Character

In a workshop I facilitated, called Recharging Realtors, I asked for a volunteer to join me at the front of the class.

Ashwani, known as Ash, a young, slim-built man, well-dressed, of Indian descent, joined me at the front of the class and stood beside me. I said to him, "Give me your superman stance." He wasn't sure what that meant, so I helped him out with these instructions.

I explained, "Stand tall, putting most of your weight on your toes with your feet about a foot apart. Cross your arms and with shoulders back push out your chest. With your chin up, stare at the door at the back of the room with your head slightly turned to the left."

Then I said, repeat after me, "I am the top producing Realtor in all of Canada; people like and trust me; buyers and sellers eagerly await to hear from me; I am the best; I love being me; I am totally Recharged; I am excited about life; I have courage and confidence!"

When I asked Ash, "How do you feel?" he had this big smile on his face. I said, "That's the way a Realtor should feel all the time." The class laughed and applauded as Ash took his seat. I could feel the energy in the room Recharge and elevate. I knew I had made an impact.

You may be thinking, this is silly, that's not me, that's not who I am!

BINGO!! . . .. that is my whole point of this exercise.

Who are you? And, is who you are working for you? Is it getting you where you want to go? Is it getting the results you seek? Or is it time to try something that works?

If you can start all over again, would you be the person that you are today?

We know we can't go back in time. Many of us may like who we are today and that is okay. However, you may not feel this way and are ready for a change.

If Ash continued this exercise every day, eventually, he would build the belief he needed to become this new character.

Notice I didn't give Ash any more skills or technical knowledge to become a better real estate agent. He already knew all he needed to know to get the job done. What I did, was give him some ideas to shift, to transform and Recharge his mindset to think and function at a higher level so he felt like a top producing agent.

Take a moment and stop reading, put down the book and stand up. Take a few deep breaths and make the Superman or Wonder Woman stance. It may seem uncomfortable; however, everything you do that is new will feel uncomfortable. That is life. Do it anyway.

This is one big step to *Recharge* for you.

Discovery Questions:

1/ Take a moment and think about what you do to rest your mind. Write out three ways you could rest your mind from the business of life. Start doing one of these every day.

____

____

____

____

____

____

____

2/ Look back and remember a time, maybe a year ago, when you were feeling anxious and worried about an upcoming event. You didn't know what the outcome was going to be. Remembering this event today, how did it conclude? Was is worth the negative energy you gave it? Is there something happening today that you can shift your thoughts to a higher more optimistic level?

____

____

____

____

____

____

____

What do you really want?

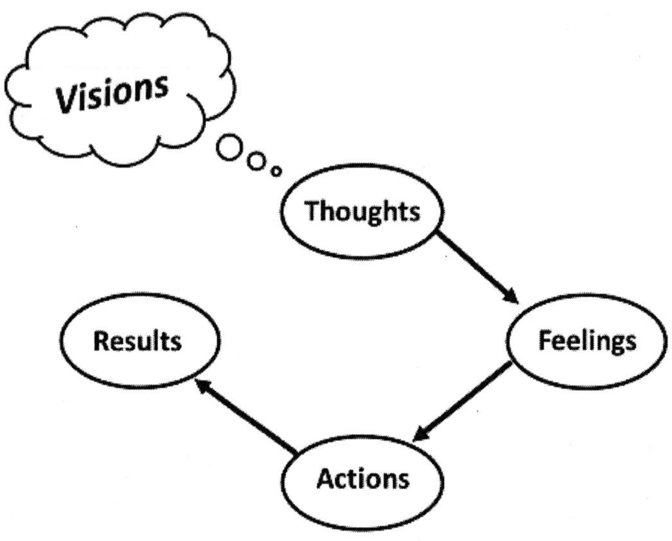

Chapter Six

What Do You Really Want?

Are You Happy?

I attended a workshop a few years back at the start of my journey of Recharge and the instructor asked this question," *What do you want? .... What do you REALLY want?"*

I thought I understood the question as my thoughts bounced from a new car, to a new job, to a bigger house and back to a new car.

She went on to say, "You can have whatever you want. Many people never stop and ask themselves this question, let alone take time to answer it."

I ended that day with a deep sense of wonder. Wondering if I was doing what I really wanted to do. This question was followed by a second question, "Am I happy?"

Take note: "What do I really want?" can be answered with, "I want to be happy."

You will see that very often what we want is something material based. A thing, a car, a house; however, to be happy is a mindset, creating a feeling. A happy feeling. An elevated emotion of joy. The same emotional state that we seek to achieve when we Recharge.

Let's define what being happy is:

Happiness is that feeling of joy that comes over you when you know life is good and you can't help but smile. ... Happiness is a sense of well-being, enjoyment, or contentment. When people are successful, or safe and secure they feel happiness.

Note: we use the word "feeling;" therefore, being happy has little or no association with the accumulation of stuff, but rather a joyful mindset creating a good feeling.

It is an interesting relationship that our social economic culture has created between the accumulation of financial wealth and being happy. The disconnect that exists is worth mentioning, and also the connection that occurs between wealth and happiness. This was an important and profound awareness I uncovered as I built the process of Recharge.

I take you back to Chapter Four, "The Box," to remind you again that we all have different paradigms and each one of us will interpret the relationship of happiness to wealth in a different way. I share with you what I have learned on my journey and through my studies.

Remember, to Recharge requires an open mind to change and creativity.

I believe happiness is a state of mind, and has nothing to do with material and financial wealth.

Will a new car make you happy? Of course it will; however, when you think it through it is very temporary.

Feelings created externally are always temporary, leaving us in constant search for the next external stimulation to cause us that moment of happiness. (Refer back to Chapter Two, "External vs. Internal Challenges.")

Recharge to Wealth

When you get up in the morning you can decide the moment your feet hit the floor whether you will be happy or not happy. It is as simple as that. A decision, but not always an easy one. You don't need to check your bank balance or ask a friend to determine your level of happiness.

You just need to make the decision, and say,

"Today, I am Happy!" "Today, I am Happy!" "Today, I am Happy!"

This affirmation works. It will start to Recharge your mindset and shift it to happy thoughts.

By digging deeper, I find that, as long as I am happy, I don't need any wealth. This is true for some people; however, I have found that there are other feelings that create happiness and joy on our life's journey. Gratitude, contentment, satisfaction, and accomplishment are feelings that create joy in living a fulfilled life.

I have found, as I teach the workshop and share Recharge, that you don't need to be wealthy to be happy; however, if you are happy and have a higher, elevated mindset, building financial wealth is accelerated. All the characteristics of a Recharged mindset are essential to building powerful relationships and attracting financial wealth.

Remember Ash in Chapter Five, a salesperson making a sales call feeling good about what they are doing. Standing tall, feeling confident, feeling proud of what they are doing. This person will outsell others that are not recharged.

A person who is feeling happy and confident will attract and create powerful relationships in business and in personal life. The positive magnetic energy that is created through being Recharged will outperform their colleagues every time.

We see examples of this around us all the time. Next time you attend a party or a gathering of people, observe where the focus of the energy is. Often there will be one person that others have gathered around. The storyteller. This person usually has the confidence and courage that Recharge creates. They are the happy influencers. They have the positive magnetic energy of Recharge.

A sales or business professional, Recharged, will create an experience for their clients and customers that causes them to want to return again and again. Does Recharge to wealth work? I am living proof.

Are there exceptions? Yes. There are people who get what they want, and achieve results through bullying. They are liked by few and respected by none, but despite their crusty approach, they work hard, push hard and build financial wealth.

I asked myself, if they were Recharged, would they have gotten bigger, faster and with less stress?

Your Legacy

The question, *"What do you really want?"*, made me think of what legacy I would leave behind for my sons and grandchildren.

I recently attended the funeral of a good friend, Don Parr. I got to know Don over the last 15 years through a coffee group that meets every Thursday morning. The group consisted primarily of retired men from Dublin Street United Church. Don had lived a good life into his 91st year.

As I sat in the still silence of the church, and listened to the emotional eulogies from his children and grandchildren, it made me mindful of what my children, grandchildren and friends might say in their eulogy at my funeral?

They spoke of what a great father Don was. A father of two daughters and a son. How he passed his Christian values on to them through his actions and his integrity. The grandchildren spoke of how Grandpa Don loved to spend time with them at the cottage and how he loved to sail his boat across the glassy lake.

Don was loved by many, had lots of friends and treated people with respect. His children talked about the lessons they learned through his guidance, and the many values he taught them.

I could tell that Don was the nucleus of the family. He set a high standard, a worthy example for them to follow.

Don lived the principles of Recharge, holding an elevated mindset, teaching gratitude and forgiveness.

"What do you really want?" Maybe, it is to leave a legacy for others to follow and pass on.

I found that the answer to this question is not something you will answer in 5 minutes at a Recharge workshop. Oh, you may come up with something, but be prepared to change it over time. It is a question that many of my students found very difficult to answer. Dig deep, take your time; it is important and well worth the time spent.

Sometimes a self-analysis is the first step. Take inventory of where you are in life right now. Are you feeling good about your career path? What is your relationship with the people around you? Look at the major pillars in life. Your spiritual, financial, relationships, health and education. What are you passionate about being, doing, and having? Take your time as you look at each one of these areas and you will start to see the picture of you. If you don't like what you see, what changes would you like to make?

Remember to acknowledge life as you become aware and

mindful of self. We are all different. If you get stuck here, start with gratitude. Being grateful Recharges your mindset so you think and function at a higher level.

Recharge will bridge the gap between where you are today and where you dream of being in the future. When you have a clear vision, a crystal-clear vision of where you dream of being, only then will you start to see your life transforming to what you want. Yes, what you really want!

If I had to pick a chapter in this book to recommend that you re-read again and again, it is this one; What do you really want? It is the key to where you want to go in life. Your ultimate purpose.

Recharge Your Goals

It would be difficult to answer the question "What do you really want?" without talking a bit about goal setting as it is a building block for achievement.

As a Real Estate Sales Agent, I was encouraged, maybe even shamed, into setting goals at the beginning of each year. I started my career with Olsen Realty, in the late 80's. They were the largest Real Estate Broker in the area at the time, with five office locations. I chose them because they were one of the few Brokerages that employed a full-time trainer with an on-going training program. Goal setting was a part of this program.

At the start of each year I would review my business from the past year. I remember taking the list and going through each transaction, documenting where the business came from. I made categories such as repeat business, new business, referral leads, open house contacts, relatives, friends and associates. As you can see the list was quite long.

By reviewing this list, I would estimate what my income

could be for the upcoming year and things I could do to increase my income; ie: make more contacts, do more open houses or network with more people.

We were encouraged to make a list of the goals for the upcoming year. If you made all this money what would you do with it? My wife and I would sit down and make a list. It would read something like this:

- A new car – as ours is five years old and it's getting old.
- Buy a rental property – we have two but another one would be good planning.
- Paint the trim on the house – paint is starting to peel
- Spend three weeks at the cottage – that would be fun
- Sell 50 homes – a number that seemed reasonable.
- Buy a new computer – one that is faster with more memory.

The list would usually be 10 top things that we would like to accomplish during the next year. Exciting!!??

After doing this for many years I realized these were not goals. This was an activity list. A shopping list requiring little or no extra effort and at the end of the year we would be pleased with ourselves because we would have accomplished 7 out of 10 things on the list. The other 3 didn't matter. I guess they were not meant to be.

Our income would be about the same every year because we did the same things every year. Our habits, systems and activities were all based around earning the same income. I never stretched my thinking or asked myself, "What do I really want?" If I want to sell 60 homes this year, what will it take to do that? Can I do 100? Why not? What would I need to do to sell 100 homes next year? Am I willing to do what it takes? Let's talk to someone that is selling 100 homes a year and learn what they are doing different than I do. Anything is possible, but I need to get out of my box and do something different. I cannot expect to get different results if I continue to do the same things.

SMART Goals

Many people don't like to set goals and so they avoid the exercise. A very small percentage of people actually write their goals down. Others write them down at the beginning of the year and never look at them again. I can only guess that this is because they were never taught how to set goals. We want to look at goal setting as a process and not an exercise with a beginning and an end.

Goals and objective setting is a huge topic, and there are many books written on the subject. However, for the purposes of Recharge I will share briefly my thoughts, and what I think is most important for you to consider right now.

To have a goal, a target, a destiny is to look at some future event, or achievement that we set our sights on and direct our effort towards.

"If you don't know where you are going, how will you know when you get there?" is a phase often used to emphasize the importance of goals and setting goals.

There are many models, systems, or templates available to assist us in reaching our goals, but the one I find most direct and appealing and endorsed by other coaches and trainers, is the acronym S.M.A.R.T., sometimes referred to as "smart goals." Following is the meaning of smart.

S - Specific – State exactly what you want. The who, what, when and where. Have a clear vision of what the end looks like. As a salesperson or entrepreneur it may be a number, an amount or quantity.

M- Measurable – Your goal must be quantifiable. Generalities don't work. You must be able to track and evaluate your progress so you can make adjustments or corrections along the way.

A- Attainable – Having goals that stretch you, challenge your paradigm and make you think outside of your box are encouraged; however, the goals must be achievable and not just hopes and wishes.

R- Realistic - Your goal must be appropriate to the current time period, or circumstances and of contemporary interest aligned with your immediate objective. It maybe relevant as a stepping-stone leading to the larger purpose. You must be willing and able.

T- Timely – Set a date on your goal. Soon, some day, are not timely or date stamped. Conditional is also a stopper for moving ahead. Example: when I retire, when spring comes, when it stops raining are all conditions. This gives up control to something or someone and it restricts our ability to move ahead.

The acronym SMART has set the foundation for goal setting for thousands of professional salespeople and entrepreneurs. It is important that you use something to aid your thought process. You must believe in what you are doing. Belief will come from doing.

Taking control, taking responsibility of "what you really want" will help you set goals that lead you to a purposeful life. The Recharge process, creating your elevated mindset, will help you have the right attitude when setting goals and making choices that lead to becoming the person you want to be.

Recharge is all about doing things differently. Shifting your paradigm. Elevating your mindset to think and function at a higher more productive level.

The Bridge

"Recharge will bridge the gap between where you are today, and where you dream of being in the future."

The bridge is what it takes to get from here, to where you dream of being in the future. I make the assumption that there is a gap, a space where something is missing, otherwise we would all know what we want, set our goals and reach them when we said we would, every time.

I believe the value and benefit in goal setting, planning out the activities and strategies, is not in reaching the goal as much as the growth we achieve and experiences we have on the journey to the goal.

One of the challenges in the journey is that we can get so bogged down in the day to day challenges that we lose sight of our end goal. This is why it is important to keep our goals in front of us, at top of mind all the time. We will talk more about that in the chapter to come; however, as an example, I carry a goal card with me wherever I go. It is not buried in my wallet or lost in my office drawer, but in my pocket where it is easy to pull out and read any time of the day.

The Recharge process asks you on a daily basis to elevate your mindset through affirmations and positive self-talk that create a winning attitude. When you take this winning attitude with you daily, to work, and out into the world, you will see your paradigm shift and the gap will start to narrow. Your creativity will increase and you will attract more sales and business opportunities.

The courage and confidence you build within you from knowing what you want, and knowing what your purpose is, will make you unstoppable.

The gap is not that you need to know more, or have better skills; it is in the mindset that you hold as you take and use this knowledge and these skills into the world and into your client relationships. Yes, you must know what you are doing, and the more skilled you are the more proficient you become; however your mindset will triumph over skill and knowledge every day because mindset is what gets you up in the morning, Recharges you and makes you soar ahead of your competition.

With a Recharged attitude, the right thoughts, the elevated, optimistic mindset, you will start to see that the circumstances you thought were holding you back will start to change. I recall a well-known phase by Wayne Dyer: "*Change the way you look at things and the things you look at change.*" You will start to function in harmony with your goals. People will see a change in you and those people who are like-minded will be attracted to you.

Let's continue the journey of Recharge and move closer to what you really want.

Discovery Questions:

1/ Create a state of happiness. Think of gratitude. Write down three thoughts you can create immediately to make you feel happy. How does your body feel? Do you feel an energy shift?

____
____
____
____
____
____

2/ Review the meaning of smart goals. Take one of your goals and apply the S.M.A.R.T acronym to it. Does your goal measure up to these criteria?

____
____
____
____
____
____

3/ Make a goal card and write on this card what you really want. Be bold, courageous and creative.

____
____
____
____
____

Chapter Seven

Reboot and Recharge

Are You a Morning Person?

I believe that how we manage the first hour of our day is very important to how we feel, the results we get, and how productive we are for the rest of the day. Are you a morning person? Do you like to get up early in the morning? Do you jump out of bed, fully charged, excited about starting a new day? Or, do you lay in bed in the morning, nodding off and on till the sun shining in the window is so bright, you can't keep your eyes shut.

I believe there are two types of people in the world. There are the morning people, and there are those that wish they were morning people.

I have found there is a direct correlation between a Recharged person and a person that starts the day early and excited about a new day.

My grand-daughter Linnie was 6 years old when we decided it was time she came for a sleepover at Grandpa and Grandma's house. We prepared the bed in the guest room for her to sleep and, after she negotiated a drink, 3 stories and a song out of Grandma, we got her all snuggled in for the night.

About 3 am. we heard this faint little voice, "Grandma, grandma, grandma," ever so softly. Linnie was standing beside our bed. "Grandma I have something to show you," she said. Reluctantly, Grandma got up and went down stairs with Linnie to the kitchen. To Grandma's surprise, Linnie had been working on crafts. Little sparkly shapes of paper and coloured card board were all over the kitchen table and stuck with tape to the refrigerator.

We have a box we call the making box, full of craft supplies that she had taken out of the cupboard in the kitchen. We can only guess she had been up for hours working away at her little projects.

Linnie had a reason to get up early. She was excited about making crafts and showing Grandma.

I tell you this story because I believe, if you're not a morning person, it's because you don't have a good reason to get you up in the morning, or you don't understand the importance and benefits of starting the day early.

A few years back I remember getting up at 4am. I got dressed and tip-toed out of the house. It was pitch black outside. I drove down to the river with my fishing pole in hand. I loved to sit by the river and watch the sun rise, listen to the sound of the running water and the chirping from the birds as they woke up one by one.

Think of a time when you woke up early, really early. You were doing something or going somewhere. The reason was big enough to get you up early. I believe sleeping in is a habit and often has nothing to do with being tired.

If your reason, what you want, is strong enough, then you can start to develop new habits that will assist you in the direction you want to go. I get up at 6am every day. I never used to until I discovered what I really want. I had to make some changes. I make sure I go to bed earlier. This works for me.

By Recharging, rebooting every morning, we elevate our mindset, we have more energy, we are excited about what we want. Are you a morning person?

Recharge Your Morning!

Hal Elrod, author of *The Miracle Morning*, talks about the importance of that first hour of your day. I believe by having a regular Recharging routine in the morning, it will transform your day and create the life you want.

Your day should start the night before. Everyone is different and everyone has a different amount of sleep requirements to maximize the energy for the next day. I look for 7 ½ hours sleep each night. To bed and sleeping by 10:30pm and up and out of bed for 6:00am. Does this happen every night? NO. This is my perfect night that I strive for. There are days when I need to be up and out of the house by 6:00am and there are days that I don't get to sleep till after midnight. It happens; don't beat yourself up. Tomorrow is a new day to start over. You find and decide what works best for you.

I schedule tomorrow, the night before. When you wake up in the morning you don't want to be asking yourself, "What should I do today?" That is too late. Your day already has started. When I drive my car out of the driveway I am not worried about where I should go! I already know or I wouldn't be driving. A well-planned day is a productive day.

This doesn't mean that we can never be flexible. Change our plans. Reschedule due to priorities shifting, or last-minute cancellations. As a salesperson and entrepreneur, we make running changes all the time. It is important to time block your day. Have a plan and work your plan at least 80% of the time;

otherwise you are putting out fires and not being productive.

I have friends and acquaintances that are employed in jobs that require them to start their day at 5:00am. Others work evenings and some work shifts, meaning they start their day at different times on different weeks. Police, firefighters, and health care workers are some examples where my schedule would not work for them. The important part is to start your day Recharged, whenever your day starts. Find a way to fit it in. It will change your life.

I call it my "Hour of Power." In this hour I have seven areas I like to work on that I feel are important to starting my day. When I get out of bed, the first place I head for is the washroom, if I didn't go there at some point through the night. Inevitably, I pass the mirror on the way, stop, take a look and often smile because I like what I see. Do you like what you see? You will by the end of this book.

Recharging your morning, your hour of power, focuses on two parts. The physical and the mental part of the body. Starting with the physical part makes the most sense as the first step is to get out of bed no matter what. Your mindset will help you, with the anticipation of the new, exciting day.

Healthy routines, and habits are essential to a successful Recharged day.

Exercise – Have an exercise routine to start your day. I have a friend and the first thing she does in the morning is to go for a 30-minute run. I have a colleague that goes to the gym first thing every morning for a workout. Whatever works for you is good. The point is to do something that will get the blood flowing. I do a stretching routine that I find very refreshing. Doing some deep breathing is effective in boosting the oxygen level in your body. This will enhance your thinking and mental activity. My wife and I like to take a walk at the end of each day when possible. Not only does this give us additional opportunity to exercise but it also provides a time when we can connect, talk about our day and things to come in days and weeks ahead. Our dream times.

Breakfast – How many times do I hear people say, "I don't have time for breakfast, I'll get something at the office." They get to work and sit at their desk with a coffee and a muffin. Wow! And this becomes a habit, the norm, and their body is starving. It throws the rest of the day off. You're hungry and end up eating more junk, not realizing what effect it is having on your day. I've done this, I've been there, I know the routine too well.

Have a healthy breakfast. For me that is a hardy bowl of oatmeal, an assortment of fruit and a large glass of water. No sugar. I am not a dietician, but this works for me. I believe that what we eat, what we put into our bodies, is a major contributor to our health and how we feel. Eating healthy is like any change you make in your life. You first must start with a conscious effort and be very intentional about what you are doing. By creating a routine, you Recharge, you develop a healthy eating habit.

One of my challenges was breakfast meetings. I love to go out for breakfast so I reviewed my choice of foods I have at breakfast and by making some changes to my choices I was able to come away feeling better and still meet my dietary goals. For example, I would choose ham over bacon or no meat at all. Eat one slice of bread, no butter, and eat ½ the potatoes or substitute them for fruit. Drink water, tea or black coffee, but never juice. By making healthy choices all day, I also reduced my weight by 40 pounds.

Quiet time – I'm sure you would agree with me that life is busy. Sometimes the busyness is not the physical running around but the busyness of mind and thoughts. We become overwhelmed with life and worry. This opens the door to anxiety and that slippery slope with a downward spiral. This is the time to start your reboot and recharge.

It is important to take and make quiet time. Even 10 minutes is better than nothing. A time when you sit in a quiet place. Be still, with eyes closed, usually sitting on a chair, focused on your breathing. In this relaxed state you are in complete control of your mind and body. In this state some people meditate, connect with a higher power, pray to the God of your choosing. It is a time of gratitude and mindfulness. Recharge will meet you in this quiet place with gifts of comfort and joy. You release all the negative, low energy thoughts and feelings from your mind and you are at total peace. A smile comes to your face. This is the perfect state to move on to affirmations.

Affirmations – When you know what you want, you can affirm it through words or self-talk. I use verbal affirmations to rechange my mindset to a higher more productive level. By using statements of "I am . . ." or "I can" we build a powerful mindset that reboots our day. An example I have used for years is, *"I weight 185 pounds and my body is happy, healthy and strong."* I started out by reading my affirmations every morning. I had 10 that I read and after a while I knew them from memory and didn't need to read them. Some of my affirmations were derived from goals that I had set. Others were statements of the character that I wanted to become; ie: a successful real estate agent, a dynamic professional speaker or an award-winning author.

There is a voice in your head that is speaking to you constantly. Listen to that voice, your self-talk. What is it saying to you? Is the message Recharging you, rebooting your morning? Is it uplifting and giving you feelings of confidence and courage?

You control this voice, and it is very important that the messages you are hearing are in line with what you really want and where you want to go.

Visualization – Whether we are aware of it or visualize all the time. We create pictures in our mind, based on the thoughts and feelings we are having in the moment. As we read our affirmations a vision is created in our minds. We see the character we want to be. Remember in Chapter Four, we visualized "The Box." A simple exercise but very powerful. If I have trouble seeing a vision, I find it helpful to watch a video or an example that demonstrates what I want to achieve. As a professional speaker I watch other speakers on stage and see myself on stage doing what they are doing. As a salesperson you can visualize sitting in front of a client, walking them through the buying process and successfully making the sale.

Take time to create the vision of the person you want to be. We have many roles in life, at home and in our profession. This exercise can be used in any situation to create an elevated mindset. Thoughts of courage and confidence create a winning attitude. I made this a part of my hour of power as an important reminder, but this strategy will be useful throughout your day.

Journaling – There are many benefits to journaling. In 1988 I started to journal in a time when I was searching for something. Life was challenging, I was in a stressful relationship and I was not happy, feeling trapped. I started journaling as a safe place to go. I was writing and sharing my thoughts on paper with no judgement or criticism. By writing out my thoughts I was freeing myself and it gave me a new awareness of my state. I was using it as a stress management and self-exploration tool. I was gaining valuable self-knowledge. I was trying to answer the question, "What do I really want?"

Today my journaling has changed. I still use it as a problem-solving tool but also as a way of creating a positive mindset to start the day with gratitude and joy. It works best when done every day, consistently when possible.

I believe there is power in the pen. Not the computer or the tablet but the pen. When you write something out on paper it requires you to think, and there is a strong connection between the mind and your pen. This consciousness reinforces what you write to what you want. Reading your affirmations is great, but writing them out every day is much more powerful. Reading my goals every day is great, but writing them out is much more powerful in helping me internalize them and making them part of my daily thoughts.

Education – Recharge is all about encouraging and promoting continuous, life-long learning. I find it refreshing and very necessary for my growth and creativity. I continually learn and educate myself. An elevated mindset is about growing and that comes with experience and education. For some of you, this is a natural thing to do. You were born with a characteristic of curiosity, a thirst for learning right out of The Box. For others, like myself, this was new and required conscious effort and daily routines to create good learning habits. I never liked to read, and now I can't get enough of it.

In my hour of power, education is the last area I go to because it is the one that can take more time. I use every opportunity of the day to learn. When I am in the car, I listen to audio books, podcasts, and yes, my car still has a CD player. There are many sources of media that you can draw from to inspire and enrich your day. Find trainers, educators and motivators that you connect with and can relate to.

Hour of Power

This hour of power changed my life, and it will change yours too. Developing new routines and new habits is not easy, but very necessary to get to where you want to go. We cannot keep doing the same thing over and over and expect to get different results. That's craziness! Life doesn't work that way.

I have shared with you what I feel is important to have in my hour of power. As I progress and grow, my priorities will shift and so will yours, as you become aware of who you are and what you really want in life. As I age and my energy shifts, I have a need to spend more time on eating healthy. It is important to keep physically active, but as I get older my body is shifting and I need to make changes to my routine to accommodate it.

I read more than I ever have, and changed from educating myself in my profession of real estate to educating myself in coaching and mentoring others in their real estate careers and personal growth through Recharge.

Recharging your mindset every morning is the key to becoming the person you want to be.

I like to compare ourselves to a computer. We turn it off at night and everything shuts down. We power it down and the lights go out. All is quiet. Not even the fan on the power supply is running. We fall into a deep sleep.

It's 6 am., time to start our day and we switch on the power. The computer will power up with the software that is in its memory, down load the programs from ram memory and when all is on and loaded will sit and idle, waiting for its next instruction.

What do we do? We get up in the morning and power up just like the computer, and if we don't change the program, we will load the same software that was there when we powered down and went to sleep.

I'm suggesting and encouraging you to power up with new software, a new program, an hour of power that works for you. An hour that will Recharge your body and mind. A program that will put you on the trajectory of what you really want in life.

The computer needs software updates and revisions, and so do we. The program we run on becomes outdated and may not be relevant any more. Our health, our relationships, people around us may change, our goals may need revising.

Remember our box is full of redundant information from our past that may not be applicable to where we want to go in life today. The hour of power may need to shift to accommodate your life transformations. I have given you some basics from which you can grow.

Begin by writing out what your morning routine is, right now. This will give you an awareness of what is working and what changes you may want to introduce. You may get up early already and just need to implement a few changes.

Now it is up to you to engage. Are you ready and willing?

Your Recharge Moment

I hope you will take a close look at how you start your day and recognize how important it is to start the day off early and with routines that Recharge your mind and body. Because this may be new to you, it will take time to introduce the changes. Be patient, but also be persistent. As you detach from the old you and start to visualize the new you, your excitement will grow and your hard work will pay off.

One of the challenges in living the life of a Recharged person is that we are constantly being exposed and bombarded by events and experiences that pull us down. That cause us to doubt our journey, question our ability and derail our direction.

Life would be easier if we stayed at home, locked ourselves in a room away from all the day-to-day stuff. Remember that life cycles and the Recharge process is there to elevate your mindset. Refer back to Chapter Two - External vs. Internal

Challenges and review.

I call it the "Recharge Moment!"

It is that moment in time when you say STOP, because you can feel that downward spiral.

You want to stop the mental erosion to your mindset. What do you do?

I have a song that I love to play called "I Just Want to Celebrate" by Rare Earth. I love the words and I love the energy of the beat. When I play it, I want to sing and dance. It helps me want to celebrate! The high energy elevates my mindset in that moment and I experience a "Recharge Moment." I feel like a rock star.

I remember attending an event by Tony Robbins, a well-known author, speaker and motivational trainer. He is known to energize the room through loud upbeat music and bright strobing lights. He gets people up on their feet, chanting loudly, strong affirmations of "I can, I will, I am" while high fiving their neighbour. He is a master of shifting your mindset in the moment. Very effective in the moment.

You can use a similar technique. Get out of your head and into your higher mindset by distracting your thoughts instantly. This can be done by focusing on something other than your stress point. You may think this is avoiding problems, but the problem will be there when you are ready to come back to it with a new Recharged mindset.

I remember a time my wife and I were having a disagreement over how to handle a family matter. The air was getting thick, the energy was high, and the voices were getting loud. Then the phone rang!

I went to where the phone was, picked it up and said hello in my "sales answering the phone voice." It was Joan, a client calling to thank me for looking after the sale of her house and how happy she was in her new home. Her gratitude melted my heart and made my day. Wow! I love when that happens.

I hung up the phone, and there was a shift. In a calm voice of gratitude, I said to my wife, "It's okay, I'm sure we can work this out. What are our choices and what would you feel is the best way of handling this situation?"

You can see what happened. The distraction allowed for a "Recharge moment." The phone will not always ring when you want it to; however, you can be aware of the downward spiral and distract your mindset.

Discovery Questions:

1/ Are you a morning person? What is one thing you can change in your morning routine tomorrow, that will affect your hour of power?

____

____

____

____

____

____

2/ What is one thing you can take out of your present diet that is not a good choice? What is one healthy choice you could add into your diet? ie: fruit or vegetables

____

____

____

____

____

3/ Describe how you would create a recharge moment in your life.

____

____

____

____

____

____

Chapter Eight

Actions Create Results

Awareness of Our Actions

One of my favourite sayings is *"If you do nothing, then nothing happens."* It seems quite simple; however, sometimes we are looking for something to happen in life, but are not taking the actions we need to make it happen. We can jump back to Chapter Six on setting goals and soon see that sometimes we make a list of things we want but, in the end, we don't achieve them. Does this mean we didn't really want them, or were we not willing to take the actions and do the work required to reach our goal and get the results we wanted? Were we willing and able to do the work?

Newton's first law states that every object will remain at rest or in uniform motion, in a straight line, unless compelled to change its state by the action of an external force.

Newton is usually referring to an object, something physical; however, we can use this analogy for our purposes as well. If we don't take the action, do the work, apply the forces needed, then we will not see the results we want.

In this chapter I want you to focus on the actions you are taking. Be aware of your daily activity. Review your past schedule and your list of activities.

We talked about the hour of power and how important it is to start your day off Recharged with a meaningful routine that reboots your mind and body. Now we want to be mindful of our actions.

Actions are what follow our thoughts and feelings in the process. We begin with the idea, the thought, the dream. These thoughts create feelings and emotions and get us excited about what we really want. We strategize and make the plan. Then we take that plan and turn it into action. If we don't take the actions needed, it could be that our emotional feelings are not strong enough.

Actions are often referred to as the activity list. The activities are usually something physical you need to do. As a salesperson you may be delivering something, or picking up the phone and making a call. The activity may not consist of a lot of mental activity; however, it is very important in the process of reaching your goal. The important part is to get it done in a timely manner, as it is part of the process.

Actions can be simple or they can require lots of effort. Persistence and self-discipline are major factors needed in order to push ahead. By always keeping your goal in mind, that thing you really want in front, your activities will be more purposeful. It is simple but not always easy.

When you need to do something that you are reluctant to do, and you are procrastinating, dragging your feet, you need that Recharge moment. Maybe you are fearful of the outcome. Maybe you are visualizing failure rather than success. Create emotional energy that will boost you ahead. With this awareness of what actions you need to take, you can alter your mindset. Have thoughts that are in line with actions that create the successful results you are looking for.

The Car Story

Following the acknowledgement that life cycles, awareness is the next most important building block to Recharge. Once you embrace awareness and are mindful of what is happening around you, then you can be conscious and start taking control of your life.

The majority of our actions and habitual behaviours run on automatic pilot. They require very little thought. We have habits and routines that we do without thinking. This creates our paradigm. Most of us are not aware of these habits. Remember the Box. We inherited many of our habits, behaviours and beliefs. Some are good and some are not so good.

One of my favourite examples, which I use in my workshops to demonstrate how we function on automatic pilot, is the car. I am assuming that most people reading this book drive a car or some similar vehicle.

The next time you are driving your car down the highway, hopefully at a time when the traffic is not too busy, observe for a moment where your hand(s) are located. Assuming one or both are on the steering wheel, watch what is happening between your hand movement and the location of your car on the road. I observed that my hand was making corrections up and down on the steering wheel, keeping the car on the road. I was not telling or consciously controlling my hand. Oh, I could jump in anytime and move the steering wheel with a conscious thought, but what was keeping the car on the road?

Do you remember getting into the car? Did you start the car and drive it away with little or no conscious effort? Maybe you were not aware of what was happening in that moment. If you are wondering what the big deal is, then remember the first time you drove a car or were teaching a young adult how to drive. As a new driver, they sit in the car and you hand them the keys. You instruct them as to which key to use, and how to start the car. Before putting the shifter into drive, you first adjust your mirrors and put your right foot on the brake.

I am sure I missed a few points, but do you see what is happening? We take an activity, learn it, and after doing it many times the routine becomes a habit and our subconscious memory takes control, it becomes automatic. If you still are skeptical about this example, then ask a friend who has a different make and model of car if you can take their car for a drive. Your awareness will kick in immediately when you sit in their car and the unfamiliar dashboard is in front of you.

I will never forget the time I was showing a real estate property to a client. I had an older model car and the young gentleman sitting in the passenger's seat asked me, "How do I put my window down? Where is the button?" I pointed to the crank on the side of the door and said, "Just turn it in a circular motion and the window will go up and down." He was amazed as he had never seen this before. The cars he was familiar with all had power windows. I assumed everyone knew how to crank a window up and down. We often take things for granted.

We function on automatic all the time, and it is only when we stop, think and become mindfully aware of what is happening, that we can change the action and create a new habit.

The car is a simple example. Observe other things you do, such as brushing your teeth, getting dressed or eating. You will notice we all have habitual behaviours. We all do things a certain way. Start to think and observe your behaviours. This will build a mindset of awareness.

React vs. Respond

The challenge we face as we Recharge is identifying behaviours that are not conducive to where we want to go or who we want to become. To change requires us to have an openness to awareness.

As we work on becoming more aware of what we think and do, and what is happening around us, we can start to see what is working and what may need shifting.

This change or transformation is sometimes referred to as a paradigm shift.

It is the process of analyzing, and becoming aware of a habitual behaviour, then changing the activity creating a shift in what we do. Through repetition we can form a new habit, and eventually the new habit will become our new paradigm. Recharge is all about elevating your mindset, making that change in thinking to a higher level.

During the process of awareness of thought and action, you will uncover a space in time between the event and the outcome. In this space, sometimes a fraction in time, we determine if we are going to react or respond. When we react, we draw directly from our box of habits and behaviours in a particular way that may or may not be favourable to the outcome we desire. Let's look at an example:

If you accidentally bumped a glass on a table, your reaction might be swift to catch it before it hits the floor and breaks. This would be a favourable reaction with potential for a good outcome.

If you are driving on a winter day where the roads are slippery and snow covered, and you need to stop quickly, your programmed behaviour might cause you to react by quickly slamming on the breaks. This could result in a loss of control of the car. This would be a situation where a quick reaction might produce an unfavourable result. An experienced driver would respond quickly, but might not break in such a manner to risk losing control.

In many cases, where we are prone to react, we would get a more favourable result by taking a moment to think and then respond, creating a more favourable outcome. Reactions can be altered over time by rethinking and responding. It is a matter of shifting habitual behaviours, becoming aware of the outcome you are getting and visualizing the outcome you want.

Taking responsibility is also a large component in making a shift. By taking responsibility you take control, which is necessary in order to make a change. People who blame others or blame their circumstances relinquish control and will not be open to making the shift needed to achieve the desired results.

Observe a person who is very reactive. They usually are very defensive, argumentative, functioning from a lower mindset of fear and uncertainty. They let their circumstance dictate how they feel, and consequentially they don't have control of their direction in life. Their level of self-awareness is quite low.

Through daily Recharge you will shift your emotional state to the higher level. You will find that when your mindset is in a place of joy and creativity you will react less from a mindset of fear and doubt. This takes practise, but over time you will respond more and more, getting the results you want.

In Chapter Ten we will discuss more about relationships and how they are affected by changing reactions to responses.

Showing Up

I learned in my sales training many years ago that 50 to 70% of the success in sales is showing up. When I first heard this, I had to laugh because showing up seemed so obvious to me. Showing up is an important part of all aspects of life, whether it be at work, with family or other relationships.

The most obvious thought of showing up is to physically be there when you say you are going to be there, or be present when the time is scheduled. We all know people who tend to be late all the time. Even when you build in a safety zone to ensure they are on time, they are late. You think it is rude, disrespectful, irresponsible and selfish. They often joke about it but do nothing to change it. What's wrong with these people? It's their paradigm. They are programmed to be late. Somewhere along the way it was put in their box and it is stuck, and everyone else around them has to deal with it.

The only way for them to change this behaviour is through awareness, taking responsibility and making a change. Sounds easy for us, but for this person it will take a willingness, desire and effort.

Recharged people are rarely late. They feel bad and apologetic when they are late. In fact, they often arrive early as they are prepared and ready to go.

Showing up physically can also be demonstrated through your physicality. How you sit or stand demonstrates the level of engagement you have with the process. Your body language can say a lot. Sit tall and show interest. Make eye contact and avoid distractions from phones and other conversations. Be present in the moment.

Showing up is also a mindset. Not only is it important to be physically there, but you must also be mentally present. The best way to do this is to come prepared. If it is a meeting, make sure you have reviewed the material ahead of time, and have some engaging questions available. A Recharged person will always come to learn more, have questions and will be there to participate and contribute relevant ideas and information to the meeting.

When I conduct a meeting or workshop, I am always the first one there. Not just to make sure the room is set up properly, but to greet the participants as they arrive and make them feel important and valued. This also plants the seed for a good level of participation and interaction in the room. You want to create a good connection and environment for learning.

I find many people attend meetings and workshops with the idea of "what's in it for me?" They sit slouched in their chair with their arms crossed, thinking about what they are going to do after the session is over. If they are not entertained, they look at the meeting as a failure. Their vibration is low and their lack of energy and involvement sucks the energy out of the room. They come unprepared and contribute very little to the meeting. I am sure this is not you, as you are Recharged.

As you can see, showing up is a collaborative effort between the presenter and the attendee. By both parties taking responsibility for their role and showing up Recharged, the odds of a successful meeting are high.

Meaningful Daily Actions

In July of 1987, I remember vividly sitting on the side of my bed at 7am and saying "I don't want to do this." I was working a job that I didn't like. I wasn't jumping out of bed fully charged. I wasn't happy where I was, and thinking about doing this for another 31 years, until I could retire, made me nauseated.

That summer I took the real estate licencing courses and by the fall I was a real estate salesperson, excited about a new life ahead. I was free to do what I wanted to every day. I was my own boss. I could come and go as I pleased, and on top of that I could make as much money as I wanted. Life was perfect.

I soon learned a valuable lesson about taking daily actions. When I had a job, working for someone else, I was required to show up and perform certain tasks, and at the end of the day I would get paid. This assured a certain amount of security and income, even though my time was not my own.

As an entrepreneur and salesperson, self-employed with total freedom, I discovered that getting up in the morning whenever I wanted to, and doing whatever I wanted, whenever I wanted, had a cost. It resulted in little to no income.

I didn't know about the hour of power back then, or even the process of Recharge, but I did learn that I had to create a routine where I would take consistent action every day.

This is what Recharge and the hour of power created for me. Having a schedule and a daily routine to follow allowed me to be productive and profitable. Repetition will shift your thoughts, allowing for you to create a new paradigm of habitual behaviours.

You must focus. Create a contract with yourself, and do the work. It is simple but not always easy. If you are having trouble then start over with "*what do you really want?*" By working on this daily, you will develop a clearer vision and direction.

In my early years of sales, my focus was on finding people who were thinking about buying, selling or investing in real estate. I knew everyone was my client because everyone had to live somewhere. I learned that I must spend one to two hours every day on looking for new clients. That was my priority every day. That was the contract I made with myself. It was my daily action.

What is that one thing that keeps your business Recharged and growing?

Make an activity list to help you flush it out. Talk to your coach, mentor or manager. Get excited about that one thing. Elevate your thoughts through visualizing great results.

Activity Tune-up

Actions are the activities that get the work done. After all the dreaming, visualizing, affirmations and planning is done, you must take action and do the work to achieve the results you want. I found that writing out the activities I do on a daily basis is an important exercise. I would make a log and record what I did every 15 minutes of the day. This would give me an awareness as to what I was doing with my time, and if I was using my time effectively and productively. In analyzing my log, I applied the following four questions to my list of daily activities. I always kept in mind, where I was going, my goals, and what I really wanted.

What am I doing that I should stop?
Answer:

Knowing what you want your end result to be, is there something you are doing right now that is not helping you get to where you want to go? For example, in my circumstances, I resigned from the property committee at the church I attend. It was a voluntary position and I found it required more time than I wanted to give it. I can always go back and do it again.
What are you doing that you should stop? Maybe now is not the right time. Maybe now is the time to give it up. This will not be easy as your paradigm is holding you back. Break through and stop it.

What am I not doing that I should start doing?
Answer:

As you create your vision of what you want, you will realize there are things you should be doing that will assist and accelerate your progress. They are necessary to start in order to move you ahead. This could be educational and marketing-related. Make a list if you have more than one, and prioritize it.

In my case it was a vision board. For years I read and talked about making a vision board. I even took a board and mounted it to a frame but never took the time to cut out pictures of what I wanted and put them on the board. This was a big motivating factor for me. Do you have a vision board?

What am I doing that I should do more of?
Answer:

There are activities we are doing right now that are working well for us, and we just need to do more. This will be possible as we have freed up some time by stopping some things we didn't need to do.

My list in this area was quite long. I always had many good intentions, but I needed to spend more time on them. As a salesperson, prospecting for new leads is often at the top of the list. Spending time with your family may be a challenge as you grow your business. My big one was reading. I had tons of books that I bought or was gifted; I just needed to spend more time reading them.

What am I doing that I should do less of?
Answer:

There are activities we love to do and they may be very necessary; however, we spend too much time on them. By reducing this time, we can free up time for adding in new, necessary activities, or activities we need to spend more time on. Again, my list had a few items on it. I drive a lot and spend time on the road. I was able to reduce this time through better scheduling of my appointments. TV watching was anther one that required some shifting of habits, but I was able to reduce this time as well, which gave me more time for reading.

Discovery Questions:

1/ Recall a time when you reacted, when it would have been more appropriate to respond. Did you take responsibility? Knowing what you know now, how would you handle the situation differently?

____
____
____
____
____
____

2/ What is the daily action, that one thing in your business that you must do every day? Is it in your schedule, and have you blocked off time to make sure it is done?

____
____
____
____
____
____

Chapter Nine

Be Accountable

Looking at Results

We have come to the end of the process. Just to recap, we started with a thought, a dream, a vision. From that Recharged energy and excitement, as a result of these generated feelings, we created a goal. We turned it into a plan of action. With the help from the hour of power, we are now at the end of a specified period of time and we can see some results. The results can be high or low, good or bad, average or exceptional, but they are our results. Try not to attach any emotion to the results, as they are simply the outcome of your planning, your efforts, and the actions you took.

Accountability is looking at the results with an analytical eye and asking, "Have I achieved the results I desired and, if not, what else can I do?" When you are accountable you take responsibility for the outcome. You have the ability to control and account for the results. You then can prepare to take the action needed, should you need to correct. Rather than focusing on the tasks required to do a job, we want to focus on results. In order to be successful, we must focus on results, not the job.

One of the aspects of goal-setting is to have a goal that is measurable and quantifiable. In some situations, this is a bit of guesswork, especially if the business model is new to you and you don't have any historical data to use as a reference point. In this situation you can make some assumptions and begin the task. At the end of the day, or period of time allotted, you can observe the outcome and make the corrections you need to your plan of action. How many times do you hear these expressions?

"That took way more time than I figured it would."

"We're done; that didn't take nearly as long as I anticipated."

The assumptions can be off and you miss your target. Recharge, take corrective action and move on.

I remember as a new real estate salesperson, I was encouraged to make phone calls every day until I had an appointment. Different trainers looked at this process differently. I could call until I had an appointment; however, the amount of time I spent calling was ambiguous. What if after 3 hours I still didn't have an appointment? Would I spend the night? What if after 15 minutes, I set an appointment? Would I get to go home early?

As you can see, there are some variables that we don't have the answers for. For example: the quality of leads I was calling. Depending on whether they were new clients or past clients, the level of success would be different. As I made more calls my level of skill improved, and that increased my success rate. The time of day I called was a factor in reaching people to talk with. Also, how many calls could I make in an hour?

It is important, when looking at the result, to be aware of the bigger picture. Know where the results came from, how they were achieved, and under what circumstances. Can the circumstances be replicated and are they duplicatable, meaning, can you do it again?

The Value of a Coach

Over the past year I have reduced my weight by approximately 40 pounds. I now weigh 188 pounds. I didn't lose the weight, as I would lose my car keys. I disposed of it as I would dispose of garbage in the trash can. I don't ever want it back. I have always struggled with weight, right from my days at the kitchen table, when I was encouraged to eat everything on my plate. My motivation to do something accelerated one day as I was watching a video of myself doing a keynote speech on stage. I know they say a camera makes you look fat, but I did not like what I saw, and I made a commitment that day to shed some pounds.

I had been writing out my goals every morning and one of the lines was:

"I weigh 190 pounds and my body is happy, health and strong."

As you may be aware by now, if you say it and write it out every day it will happen. I was chatting with Keith, an accountant friend of mine, at a networking event and he happened to mention in conversation that he was down 25 pounds. My first response was, "Wow, that's great! How did you do that?" He told me about Weight Watchers. He invited me to attend a meeting as his guest. The group was friendly and non-judgemental, as we were all there for the same reason; to shed some weight and develop new, healthier eating habits. At that time, I weighed in at 228 pounds and felt heavy. My clothes were tight and I was starting to buy the next size up.

I share this with you because I know I would not have achieved my goal without Keith opening the door for me, and for the coaching and encouragement I received from the staff at WW. The program is Recharged with a higher mindset. Everyone wants to succeed. Not only did they talk about eating healthier, but they encouraged more movement, some form of exercise, and focusing on the goal. Why do you want to lose weight, and what are the benefits you will realize when you reach your goal?

Along with the coaching came the accountability. Each day I would keep a record of what I ate on an app on my smart phone. The app assigned points to the foods I chose to eat. It would accumulate the points and let me know when I was approaching my allotted number of points for the day. I would weigh in once a week to see the results. I could see by my results if I ate over my point limit, and make the appropriate corrections for the next week.

Coaching was the catalyst I needed to achieve greater results. I found that a good coach believes that the individual always has the answer to their own problems, but understands that they may need help to find the answer. The coach brought out the best in me and provided me with the relevant training and guidance that I needed.

Everyone in the group had different challenges. The coach encouraged us to share what was going on in our lives, what obstacles we faced on our way to reaching our goal, and what was working well for us.

Over the life of my real estate career I've had many coaches. If you look at successful athletes, they all have a coach. This person is invaluable to your journey to success. I cannot say enough good things. In Recharge, your coach will not only give you encouragement but will help you raise your mindset to a higher, winning status. They will keep you on track and accountable, and bring out the best in you. Is it time for you to consider having a coach on your team?

Coaching for Life

There are coaches for all aspects of life. Anytime you want to excel and achieve greater results at something, you should consider a coach. My experience with coaches is varied, as the field of coaching in the last 10 years has exploded and anyone can be a coach or have business cards printed with "coach" on them. You can become a certified coach after a weekend workshop. I find the saying "You get what you pay for" does not apply to coaching. There are coaches that charge thousands of dollars and give very little value or guidance, and those that are passionate about coaching and undervalue their programs. When looking for a coach, do your homework. Ask around for referrals. Read and follow up on testimonials. Make sure that you are compatible with the coach and like their style, and that your Recharged energy is in harmony. Here are a few of the coaches to consider in different areas:

A *Life Coach* is the most general of coaches. It is a person who counsels and encourages clients on matters having to do with careers, transitions or personal challenges. Life coaching is different in nature from giving advice, consulting, counseling, mentoring and administering therapy. They help you grow by analyzing your current situation, and identifying the limiting beliefs and obstacles you encounter. They help you look into your paradigm with a different perspective for getting unstuck and moving forward.

A *Fitness Coach* is usually associated or employed by a gym or fitness centre, and is hired to help individuals with physical health and fitness. They will show you exercising techniques and strategies unique to your needs and body strength. They are there to encourage you and make you accountable, and will push you to stretch outside your comfort zone. Their objective is to assist in helping you reach your pre-determined fitness goals.

A *Financial Coach* is all about helping you manage your money and assets. This area has a few sub-sections; therefore, you may consider more than one individual in this category. A financial planner may work more with investments, insurance and retirement strategies. You may have a financial advisor that will assist you with managing credit and debt. A tax advisor is also part of financial coaching. They can help and recommend tax strategies that best fit your income level. For those of you having real estate investments or real estate rental properties, I would recommend you put a real estate agent on your team to coach you and keep you informed on market trends.

A *Business Coach* is a necessity when launching your own business. As a salesperson or entrepreneur you may know your product, have the skills, and can generate high income, but you also need to know how to manage your business. A coach will help you recharge and clarify what you want your business structure to look like, based on your vision and goals. They will coach you on growth, when to hire, when to expand, when to delegate or build a team. I fell into the trap of wanting to do it all myself. My money paradigm looked at hiring an assistant as an expense rather than a source of income. If you don't have an assistant, you become one. The best advice I received was to treat my sales career as a business, not a job.

A *Recharge Coach* is necessary to empower you to Recharge every day so you have a clear vision of what you really want. Having the right mindset is so important to the balance of your life and the success of your business. This coach is someone to guide you on how to think, have a positive mindset and be a happier, more productive person who is in harmony with the new recharged you. The awareness of your paradigm, and helping you make that shift, is the number one priority of the Recharge Coach.

Mentoring

There is a difference between coaching and mentoring, although I have noticed that many people use the terms interchangeably. It was brought to my attention that the difference is that a coach usually charges for their service whereas a mentor is often free. This may not always apply.

Both coaching and mentoring are processes that enable individuals to achieve their full potential. Both will facilitate the exploration of needs, motivations, desires, skills and thoughts to assist the individual in making real, lasting change. Both coaching and mentoring have development techniques that utilize the skills of listening, questioning, clarifying and reframing. Sharing one-to-one conversations is the main way to interact in order to enhance an individual's skills, knowledge and work performance.

We previously looked at examples of coaching, and some of the areas where a coach would be utilized. Now let's explore what a mentor is, and how they fit into your growth journey.

Mentoring is a long-term process based on mutual trust and respect. It is more focused on creating an informal relationship between the mentor and mentee. This could be a father-son, or employer-employee relationship. Mentors are successful or knowledgeable people who share their years of wisdom to provide insight and guidance to entrepreneurs who encounter challenges along their journey. The mentor is usually available to respond as issues arise, and they may not meet on a regular basis. They may not have expertise in the mentee's field, but they understand how to navigate business in general.

I realized I had mentors throughout my life but never labeled them as such. I never went to them and formally asked, "Will you be my mentor?" It just happened because of circumstances. This may not always be the case. There may be a person that you trust and respect, and you would like their insight. There is nothing wrong with approaching them with the idea of building a mentoring relationship. Ask questions, ask for their opinion and input on ideas you have, and how they would handle things. You will soon know if this relationship is working, based on how you feel. If they are encouraging and give you information that is helpful, relevant and inspires you, then this could be the start of a healthy relationship. If they leave you feeling exhausted and beat up, you may want to rethink the continuation of them as a mentor.

I realized later in my life that one of the people that mentored me a lot in my early years was my father-in-law. He was the general manager of a large industrial rental company in the area, and had a lot of street smarts when it came to business. His employees liked him. He built strong relationships in the industry and was known for his honesty and integrity. He was a person you could trust.

We would often go fishing in his boat for hours. Sometimes we would sit out on the water in the quiet of the morning fog, and not a word was said. Other times we would have deep discussions on family, work, or plans for the future. Marvin has since passed; however, looking back I see now how he was a mentor to me. Think about who the mentors are in your life. Yes, there could be more than one.

You may also have had the rewarding experience of being a mentor to someone else. If you have knowledge in a specific area of expertise, offer to help others that you connect well with. If they are receptive to your thoughts, then share them. If you approach them as a know-it-all, you will repel them, and they will not be open to your input.

The Mastermind

What is a Mastermind? It is a peer-to-peer mentoring concept used to help members solve their problems with input and advice from the others within the group. The concept was created in 1925 by author Napoleon Hill in his book *The Law of Success*, and described in more detail in his 1937 book, *Think and Grow Rich*.

The Mastermind consists of a small group of like-minded people, business owners, entrepreneurs or salespeople who meet on a regular basis. The group is usually 5 to 8 members, and they should meet consistently, weekly or biweekly as preferred. If the group is too small, it loses its momentum and may not be dynamic enough to keep members' interest. If the group is too big, it loses its intimacy, and the meetings get too long, unruly and more difficult to keep focused. Meeting face to face is always preferred; however, many groups are now meeting by phone, online through audio-video connections or chat rooms. Online is great as it allows for members to be geographically anywhere in the world and still connect.

The people in the mastermind are all Recharge advocates, having a higher mindset. This brings great energy together, fostering creativity, encouragement and a positive, inspiring space. It is a great space to tap into your higher source, your spiritual dimension.

If you are joining or starting a group, you want to make sure the members in the group are at least at the same peer level as you, or even one step above you. Maybe they are already where you want to be. This is important for your personal growth and mentoring.

It is necessary to have a structure to follow at each meeting. This allows the group to be organized and efficient, where everyone has an equal opportunity to share and learn. Also, with an agenda that is followed regularly, any member of the group can lead the meeting. Rotating the leadership is recommended to share responsibility, and gives everyone an opportunity to advance their leadership skills. It is easy for the conversations to digress and drift off topic. The leader is there to flag this moment and direct the conversations back on track.

It is my experience that the best time to Mastermind is in the early morning. This will depend on the makeup of the people in the group and what their schedules are. It is very important that everyone involved commits to showing up. Now and then doesn't work. "When I can" doesn't work. You must commit to contributing to the group to get benefit from the group. Remember, showing up is over halfway to success.

The Mastermind Format/Agenda

Opening remarks - Begin with a welcome and the reading of the purpose of the group: a statement of intent that reminds everyone that they are gathered to provide motivation, accountability and information that will be a catalyst to elevate their business to the next level. This is achieved by following a pre-determined schedule used at every meeting to ensure structure and fairness amongst participants. The leader can read the opening or can delegate it to someone else within the group. It is important to make sure everyone is involved and invested in the success of the Mastermind. This is also a good time to remind the group about etiquette, respect for each other, and confidentiality of information shared within the group.

Wins - The leader then asks each member to take one to two minutes to share any wins they have had since the last meeting. A win is something good or great that happened, such as reaching a goal or milestone in their business, or something they are grateful for. It is important to monitor the sharing times as the storytellers in the group will monopolize a lot of the time. The purpose of sharing wins is to Recharge and raise the energy in the group, to congratulate successes, recognize effort, and encourage growth and progress.

Challenges – In this session the leader asks each member how the group can help them, or share something with the group where they are stuck or having difficulties in managing an event where they lack knowledge or skill. Many people are not used to asking for help, making this session more challenging for some; however, this is where the gold is. This is where you have an opportunity to tap into the energy and creativity of the group. One by one, each person shares their challenge of the week. After each person shares, then each member of the group volunteers their experiences and advice. This is the longest part of the Mastermind, as there is often discussion. Again, it is important to always be cognizant of the time.

Actions – As the final section of the Mastermind, each member shares what actions they are going to take in the next week or timeframe they are working with, to move them closer to their goal. It may be a small step or it may be a big step in the process. The purpose is to commit by verbalizing to the group what that action is. This will make them accountable to the group.

This is a brief outline about Masterminds, and how they can be a vital part of your *Recharge* process. There are many books and online references to what a Mastermind group should consist of, and the many benefits from it. For me, it is another step towards building a community of like-minded people who together mentor each other and achieve much greater results than they could on their own.

Discovery Questions:

1/ Do you have someone you are accountable to? What does this look like, and can you improve on it by formalizing the time and structure?

____

____

____

____

____

____

2/ Who in your life has been a mentor to you? What are some of the areas where this mentorship has been helpful to you in navigating through life?

____

____

____

____

____

____

Chapter Ten

Relationships are the Key

Relationships and Recharge

A relationship is defined as the way in which two or more people or groups behave toward each other. For the purpose of Recharge, we are looking at how people relate. There can be relationships between any two parts of something, not just people. We interact with people all the time, creating a relationship. It is difficult to do anything, go anywhere, buy or sell something without some type of interaction with others. It may be very brief; however, it only takes a moment of interaction to create a connection, and that connection creates a relationship.

When we think of relationships, we often think of two people. The relationship could be romantic or sexual in nature, or a friendship or relationship with a colleague we work with. These connections can have many different degrees of intensity. Typically, a relationship starts at a connecting point, a meeting point, and develops from there. We build a relationship. We improve a relationship. We create a relationship into something of value, often with purpose. The value is measured in the feelings we have, and is developed through the connection. As we develop and nurture a relationship through sharing of information and investing time, we build an increasing level of trust and good feelings towards the person(s), creating a favourable connection. There are many purposes for pursuing a relationship. They could be related to business or pleasure.

I like to think I am a people person. I am very aware of others around me, and I observe how others communicate both verbally and non-verbally. I like to connect with people and have a great interest in what people do, the stories behind them and how they got to where they are in business and in life. When I meet someone new, I love to ask probing questions, and sometimes feel like I am conducting an interview. Some people are quite open and free about sharing their story, and others are reserved and more cautious about open conversation.

As you become Recharged and start to be more aware of who you are and where you want to go in life, you will also develop a heightened awareness of others around you. You will become more in tune to conversations, and discern what information is adding to your wellbeing. You will easily pick out of a crowd those individuals that are in harmony with your Recharged mindset.

I remember the day I drove my brand new 1995 Toyota Corolla off the lot. It was the very first new car I had ever owned. It looked and smelled amazing! I loved that car.

It wasn't long before I noticed other people were buying and driving Toyota Corollas just like me. As time passed it felt like everyone was copying me. They were all over the city. Why were there suddenly all these Corollas on the road?

The reality was that, yes, the car was popular; however, there weren't more Corollas on the road; I was just aware of them, and every time I would see one, a flag of awareness would go off in my mind.

I'm sure this has happened to you. Maybe not with a car, but something else you may have thought was unique and suddenly they were all around.

Start being more aware of the people around you. Are they Recharged? Are they people you want in your close circles? Are they someone you would like to get to know?

Be a Cheerleader

I believe building great relationships is one of the most important things we can do in life. To me there is no value in accumulating great wealth and having lots of assets (stuff) if you don't have someone to share it with.

An important part of Recharge is sharing your elevated energy, that state of joy and gratitude with others. This can be done intentionally or unintentionally. You become an advocate for people. You become their cheerleader.

As Recharge takes hold in your life, you will feel better about where you are going and what you want. You will wake up in the morning with purpose and direction. Your awareness of who you are and your focus on your direction will increase. In this new state, this new paradigm you have created, you will find opportunities for new and better relationships.

The new you will start to be noticed by those around you. Your new energy and your new vibration will unintentionally affect people around you. People close to you will notice a change. Some will enjoy it immediately and find it refreshing, while others will be skeptical about the shift. How you feel and function in this new space will be observed by others. Be aware of this but don't react to it. This new you becomes the new normal for you. You will become a cheerleader for those around you.

Being a cheerleader may not be something that is in your box or something you've learned at the kitchen table when you were young; however, it is something you can learn now. At this moment you may be thinking to yourself, "That's not me! I can't do that! I'm the quiet reserved type."

Great, I am not asking you to make huge personality shifts. I am suggesting that you start taking small steps toward being a cheerleader. Remember you are Recharged, and have a new direction. The first step is to acknowledge and affirm that you can do this. Second, be aware of the opportunities as they arise, and last, get excited and take action.

Start with small intentional changes, to encourage others. Congratulate others on their accomplishments. Compliment others on their clothes. Encourage colleagues when they struggle with large challenges. A cheerleader brings a higher level of energy into the room with their enthusiasm. This vibration is contagious, and you can shift the whole room with goodness, grace and gratitude. Remember, this is about you helping others Recharge. It's about building relationships and better connecting with others.

I'm sure you have met that person in your life who is full of energy, with a smile on their face most of the time, and always asks how you are doing. Watch and be aware of the little things this person does. How they interact, how they respond vs. react. They are excited but calm. Friendly but respectful. Interested but not intrusive.

As you become a cheerleader for others and a new community is formed around you, you will be aware of others in your life that are your cheerleaders. Yes, these are the people who come to you with support and encouragement. Their energy elevates you in that moment, and together you Recharge each other. Yes, you can be a cheerleader!

People

I sometimes go to the mall for a walk if I am feeling off, just to be around people. People give me energy and help me Recharge. They are also a source of entertainment and amusement. I will sometimes sit on a bench in the mall and watch people walk by. Some with young children and others with babies. Some are older and some younger. I watch their faces and see the many levels of energy. From a happy, joy-filled smile to a serious purpose-driven stare, and all the faces in between.

I developed an awareness to a point where after spending only a few minutes with a person, I knew if they were Recharged, had a dream, or were stuck in the sea of sameness, comfortable in that space of mediocrity. They may have natural abilities that were never uncovered and developed.

Because of the strong importance I place on relationships with others, getting to know how other people function and think became a high priority for me. I learned that nurturing strong relationships is the key to opening doors to greater opportunities to share my *Recharge* message, and build wealth to do more for others. This also presented another challenge.

If you recall, I began Chapter One of this book with the acknowledgement that people are all different. When I embraced the values of Recharge, I was naive to think that this was for everyone, or that everyone would be excited and embrace my program. The truth surfaced very quickly, and I realized that not everyone was looking for more out of life. I wanted to Recharge the world, but realized that the world didn't want to be Recharged.

There is an elephant in the room that we don't want to talk about. It is the idea that some people are comfortable where they are. Some people are afraid to shift their paradigm and do things a different way. The fear of changing is bigger than the reward. Their dream, if they have one, is not big enough and so the Recharge never takes hold.

Many people have circumstances that dictate who they are and who they become. Their environment holds them hostage, not allowing for growth outside the boundaries of their BOX. Their habits and daily routines are such that they have no desire to expand and build new relationships. If you asked them if they are happy, they would say yes, as that is what they are programmed to say. If you asked them if they are doing what they want to do, they would say "Yes," or "What else would I do?"

Don't misunderstand me. I am not discounting or putting this mindset down; however, if they knew they had a choice, would their life change?

The world is filled with people from all walks of life, and as you expand your thinking and build new relationships you will encounter Recharged people. They are in all races and cultures. You will spot them in business, in the shopping malls, and in your spheres of influence. They will be at church, associations, schools and community groups. One by one you will connect and meet the influencers.

Learn to love and appreciate people, and start to become aware of the people around you.

The Key is Letting Go

I remember hearing these words at an inspiring, personal growth seminar one Saturday afternoon:

"If it was easy, then everyone would be doing it."

It was the statement I recalled when I would get frustrated with the attitudes and behaviours of people around me. I was taught not to judge people, and to accept others for who they were, but at times I found this very difficult to do.

Everyone has a different journey and different stuff in their box to deal with. We all have different paradigms that direct our habitual behaviours. I wanted those I loved and were closest to me to think and act like me. I wanted to help them Recharge and feel better about life. I wanted them to feel the gratitude and joy of a new positive mindset. Yes, I wanted them to change and be something different than they were.

I learned many years ago, we never want to be frustrated because someone doesn't behave, function or react the way we want them to. This is a no-win situation and can only lead to never-ending worry and anxiety. These are negative feelings that rob us of the creativity and self-awareness of a higher mindset.

I recall a client and good friend, Jack. He had difficulties maneuvering through life. A marriage breakdown, infidelity, bankruptcy, along with depression and emotional rollercoaster, all contributed to a person that in my eyes never grew up. Jack was financially challenged and would always spend more then he made, leaving him always in debt. I learned over time that Jack's box was filled with difficult memories from the past, and his experience at the kitchen table was not encouraging and supportive.

I recall Barb, another acquaintance, who I would meet on occasion for coffee. She was impulsive, high-strung and loved to talk. A single mom of three. Her favourite topic was her ex-husband, who up and left her and moved in with her best friend. It sounds like a classic murder mystery novel, without the murder.

There are more people and more examples, but I think you get the picture. Each time we would get together, the pattern was the same. They would dump their story, and I would take it in and leave feeling frustrated, exhausted, drained, like the energy had been sucked out of me. I would try to offer advice, coaching tips to help turn things around for them; however, their circumstances were such that they couldn't see past the blame. They were victims and refused to, or didn't know how to, take responsibility. I was feeling a strong disconnect, and each time we got together it was less enjoyable for me.

I tried to stay emotionally detached from each situation and just be a good listener. After all, they were not my problems. I wanted to help but I couldn't. One of the most difficult things I ever did was to disconnect from a friend. It was hard to do, but necessary.

There will come a time in life when you will need to let go, cut the ties and move on. As I grew stronger in my belief of the Recharge process, I could see they didn't get it. I knew I had to let go or their behaviour would take me down. The key was to let go.

Sales Relationships

There are many different types of salespeople, selling a variety of products and services. We can break them into two categories for the purposes of this example. There is the passive salesperson, and the aggressive salesperson. Some may use other words like soft and hard. Let's look closer at the differences, how they interact with people, and what opportunities are available for a Recharged salesperson to develop relationships.

In the real estate sales business, we would look at the two differences this way: Are you going out and getting the business, or are you waiting for the business to come to you?

For example, a passive sales situation would be if you are

sitting in the office waiting for the phone to ring, or hosting an open house waiting for someone to come in and talk to you. In an active sales approach, you would make calls to people and ask them if they are thinking of buying or selling real estate in the near future. You might go and knock on some doors in your neighbourhood to find clients.

In the passive approach you can't always predict or control the number of clients you talk to, and are relying on the possibility of clients coming to you. This makes it more difficult to control your income, other than using historical stats based on past results.

Why would someone pick a passive approach over an active approach?

Good question. More people will pick a passive approach because it takes less effort. Their goals are smaller and they settle for a lot less in life. Lower risk, lower rejection and lower income. I have encountered many people in passive positions that are Recharged with a positive mindset and are excellent at building great relationships with clients. They sometimes stay in these positions because they lack the confidence, courage or desire to reach for more. This isn't a bad thing. It just is where they are at, and that is okay.

A Recharged person with a goal of making a certain number of sales, or a higher level of income, will find passive sales frustrating, and will likely not be happy with this arrangement. A Recharged person will want the opportunity to increase their sales ratio through better connecting with the client. A higher mindset creates a friendlier, fun sales experience.

Most Recharged salespeople will choose an active or aggressive approach to sales. They will choose to go after the sale rather than sit and wait for the sale to come to them. They can control the number of contacts they make, and the number of clients they develop into sales. More sales translate into higher income.

By elevating your mindset, you can increase your sales. Your why, that came from your what, gives you a purpose, and from your life's purpose you develop strength, confidence and courage. The skills and knowledge you learn when you start off are similar on both approaches. The difference is your attitude or the gap. That winning attitude, with the repetition of activity, will develop your knowledge and skills to a higher level, increasing your level of service to your clients.

This higher level of service you provide becomes habitual. This will result in you attracting not only more clients, but a better quality of client. A client that is in harmony with the new you. This works! I have seen and experienced it many times. You build a client relationship that will last a long time. They like and trust you, and often refer you to their family, friends and colleagues.

Building Community

In the fall of 2019, I attended an event by Bob Proctor, a Canadian author, entrepreneur, and motivational speaker on mindset and shifting your paradigm. As I looked around the room of several hundreds of people, I saw how mesmerized the audience was with his message. The energy in the room was high, and the message was well-received. It was as if everyone in the room was connected and on the same vibration. I felt that a community of Recharged people were in this room. There was a feeling of fellowship. Those attending shared common attitudes, values, interests, and beliefs.

I came home that weekend feeling a sense of community, where everyone there had common characteristics.

I learned that it is important to build a community of recharged people who have common attitudes, and a desire to live a similar life, seeking a higher mindset. By building a community, I would create a support system not only for myself but for those I connect with.

I talked in an earlier chapter about the importance of a coach and mentor, and also in this chapter we mentioned about being and having a cheerleader. These are all parts of building a community. We also talked earlier about having a Mastermind of like-minded people meeting on a regular basis to share and support each other. Learning as a group is so much more powerful than on your own, as you can hear other people's perspectives on various topics. This will open your mind to a new and more creative way of thinking. We make changes, paradigm shifts, in our life by looking at things from a different perspective. Change creates opportunity for growth and personal development.

I emphasized earlier in this chapter how important it is to develop great relationships. A supportive community is the result of well-developed relationships. No one can build or create anything big without having a team of supporters, associates or colleagues around them.

I see more salespeople and business entrepreneurs assembling a team of experts to achieve things they could never have done on their own. These are individuals who have specialized training in specific areas. If you recall in Chapter Nine we looked at the many different types of coaches a person could have, depending on their needs. Building a team is very similar, where you employ individuals to do specific tasks that you can't do, don't have the time to do, or that don't make economic sense for you to do.

I have felt the rapid change in technology over the past ten years has left me falling behind. For many years I would learn the minimum I needed to know for the task at hand. As you know, doing the minimum will not put you at the head of the class, and so I found myself and my business sliding. I didn't have the desire to learn systems in more depth, and I found a negative cloud over me in regard to technology. Remember, I am a people person! I lifted that dark cloud when I delegated my technological needs to my new assistant. What a relief! I still have to maneuver around the apps on my smart phone; however, I can handle that with a new, Recharged attitude.

Build your community, build your team. Don't try to do it all by yourself.

Discovery Questions:

1/ Take inventory of the people around you. How can you be a better cheerleader for them?

____
____
____
____
____
____

2/ Is there someone in your life that you should consider letting go of? Why? How do you plan on making this happen and when?

____
____
____
____
____
____

Chapter Eleven

Opening New Doors

Your Paradigm

Of all the things that will hold you back in life, your paradigm is number one. It will keep you where you are today instead of where you dream of being in the future. It will prevent you from opening doors to new opportunities. It will make your *Recharge* process more challenging.

Your paradigm is the way you look at something. It is your standard, your perspective, your set of ideas. A paradigm is your frame of reference. Your paradigm is how you see the world, based on all the information that you have gathered, and the beliefs that you possess. If the universe is compared to a computer processor, a paradigm is like the operating system. It is what is in your Box.

Paradigms are important because they define how we perceive reality, what we believe. As such, everyone is subject to the limitations and distortions produced by their environment and life's experiences.

A paradigm shift is when we change the way we look at something. It is a change in our perception or belief. We see things from a different perspective. This can happen through an experience, through education and study, or through a major emotional event where there is a shift in the fundamental approach or underlying assumptions.

Paradigm shift is a change from one way of thinking to another, and can apply to anything on earth – your job, your married life, your relationships, your home, your surroundings, and more importantly, your mindset or attitude.

One of the most memorable events in my life was that of 9/11. It produced one of the most notable and dramatic paradigm shifts of my generation. I vividly remember that morning, and where I was as the events unfolded. It was on September 11th, 2001, when two planes, American Airlines Flight 11 and United Airlines Flight 175, were crashed into the North and South towers of the World Trade Center complex in Lower Manhattan, New York. This was two of four coordinated terrorist attacks on the United States that day.

As a result of this event, we had a major change to our country's security, and how we view the world and its continual war on terrorism. Our mindset and memories have shifted forever. If you remember this time in history then you will relate to the huge impact it had on people's lives for generations to come. This was a major paradigm shift to our belief system, and how we view the world. It eroded the safety and security of people in their own cities within the United Sates.

9/11 opened the doors to new thinking and new strategies. Even though 9/11 was a catastrophic event that devastated and saddened the world for many years, it also opened our eyes and made us aware of how fragile and vulnerable life is. It was a day I will never forget.

Thousands of people died and millions of people were dramatically affected by the event. Families, jobs, and lives were changed forever. Devastating memories were created that would have long-term effects for years to come.

In *Recharge* we look for the good in everything. We reach for the higher mindset; we take the higher road and think about the lessons we can learn. Sometimes this is not easy, and it requires a mind shift that you may not be willing to make in the moment. Only as time passes are we able and willing to see the positive effects that were created.

The events of 9/11 created many changes in the world. There was a new awareness to the possibility of future terrorist attacks in North America. Security protocol was changed at the airports and border crossings. Construction methods were reviewed and questioned, seeing how the twin towers crashed to the ground in the heap of rubble. 9/11 created an escalating war on terrorism throughout the world.

Embrace the Uncomfortable

As I power up every morning and *Recharge* the new day, I create a mindset to embrace the uncomfortable.

We as human beings strive to be comfortable, to be wealthy and stress-free. We tend to avoid anything that makes us feel awkward, uneasy, or uncomfortable.

Doing things outside of the box is usually referred to as doing something new, different, uncomfortable. It is important to know that we learn and grow in this uncomfortable zone. If you live in the comfortable space all the time, you miss out on growth.

If you recall, you can't coast through life. You are either growing or dying. The reality is that a person who is growing is continually in the uncomfortable zone. Think of all the things we do in life that cause us to stretch and grow. We exercise every day to strengthen our bodies; we learn new computer programs because technology is constantly changing; we read every day to learn more life skills. The list is endless. Every time we make a change, and shift that paradigm, we grow. This is the essence of *Recharge*.

I learned this profound lesson and I share it with you. In order to grow and achieve what you really want in life, you must enter the uncomfortable zone. Every day I push myself to do something uncomfortable. By doing this I am growing every day. *Recharge* is about stretching, growing and shifting your paradigm a bit every day. The more you enter and challenge your comfort zone, the easier it becomes. Yes, it becomes easier to do the uncomfortable and that propagates a growth mindset.

Your new growth mindset becomes the new habitual behaviour, and you start looking for the uncomfortable space because that is what feeds you, as this is your new paradigm.

I find that, in every situation, I look for opportunities to learn, contribute and grow. Knowing that growth is the catalyst to opening new doors, doing things that may be uncomfortable becomes easier to embrace.

Did I use the word easy? For some of us, it is anything but easy, as we are all different and have different stuff in our boxes. Taking on activities that are in the uncomfortable zone is far from easy. For the first while you may say no to opportunities that arise. The shift may be too big for you. Your old paradigm is too strong. It is okay to say no a few times. Don't beat yourself up. It is a process, and each time you will grow stronger until the day you say yes to most things.

I believe that there is no such thing as "an opportunity of a lifetime." You will be presented with opportunities every day of your life. If the timing isn't right for you, then wait for the next time. Just as the sun comes up every day, so too is the flow of opportunities to you every day. Expect them!

By developing a mindset of expectations, you will be mindfully aware of *Recharge* all the time. Expect a miracle to happen. Expect good things to happen every day.

Have you had a day where everything went perfectly? This wasn't an accident or coincidence. Be aware that there are good things happening around you all the time. Awareness will connect you with them so they flow towards you, continually opening new doors.

Visualize the Door

For as long as I can remember, I wanted to be a professional speaker. I wanted to travel all over the world: Paris, London, Singapore, Boston, New York, Toronto and Sydney to name a few. I had a vision of walking onto this huge stage, like that of Carnegie Hall in New York. It was brightly lit with three large video screens across the front, displaying my name and picture with the caption, *"Master of Recharge."*

The world would now hear my message! The crowd was on their feet applauding, hooting, whistling, loud and enthusiastically as though they knew what message was coming. The music was rocking the room. There were thousands of people. Eventually the cheers quieted, the audience took their seats and there was silence in anticipation of my opening words.

They were waiting for the message of *Recharge*. They were waiting for a life-changing experience.

This is my vision, the movie I play on the screen of my mind, every day.

What does your movie look like? Are you the leading character?

As you play your movie on the screen of your mind, over and over every day, it becomes clearer and you will see more detail, even colour! It is a good idea to write it out in detail so you increase your awareness of what you want and what you see. In Chapter Six we talked about "What do you really want?" Now, let's look at the doors that will open for you as you pursue what you really want.

This may sound magical, not possible, but remember I said "Expect a miracle." Take what you are thinking right now and spin it around 180 degrees. The complete opposite to your present thought. Think *what if*?

It is possible, now it's up to you. Are you willing? Plant the seed and start playing your movie.

As your belief builds and your awareness of what you want increases, doors of opportunity will start to present themselves all around you. I started being aware of speaking opportunities in my area. Not only did I speak at my Toastmaster club and other Toastmaster clubs in other cities nearby, but I opened doors to speak at service clubs like Rotary. A door opened at Re/max, giving me opportunities to speak about *Recharge* to new Real Estate salespeople.

Word spread and I started to attract bigger and better speaking opportunities. As I told people what I was doing, the community of people kept expanding.

I noticed that more and more doors of opportunity presented themselves to me. I learned a lesson quickly. The more I said YES to opportunities that arose, the more other doors of opportunity would open. However, if I said NO to an opportunity then fewer doors would open. Say YES to as many open doors as you can that lead in the direction you want to grow.

In my case I would sometimes see a door and, even though it was not open, I would knock on it, ask and see if there was interest or speaking possibilities for me. Asking will open doors for you.

In *Recharge* we stimulate your creative mind by elevating your mindset. A creative mind will open new doors that you may not have been aware of prior to *Recharge*. Expect to foster a new environment of opportunity. Manifest through visualization, things, events and experiences you desire.

The Vision Board

What is a vision board and how does it work?

Throughout this book I have had many opportunities to share the tool of the vision board with you. We visualized the Box; we saw ourselves around the kitchen table, we stood like Superman, a top real estate salesperson in our office. I waited until now, for as I approach the end of this book, it will help you sustain your new direction and keep you recharged in times ahead.

A vision board is a tool used to help clarify, concentrate and maintain focus on what you really want in life. It is a collage of images, pictures, and affirmations of your dreams and desires, designed to serve as a source of inspiration and motivation. It uses the law of attraction.

The vision board will provide you with a daily visual reminder of your dreams and goals, and help you with keeping a recharged, positive, elevated mindset.

The reason that vision boards work so well is because you see them every day. Visualization is one of the most powerful, popular and effective mind workouts that you can do.

I created my vision board from a piece of bristol board that I purchased at the dollar store. I chose to mount it on a wooden frame that I constructed because I wanted to be able to move it around, as in the beginning I wasn't sure where it would be most effective. You don't need to frame it.

For a long time, I didn't know what I wanted to put on my vision board so it sat empty for months. At one point I even misplaced it. I thought about a picture of a new car or a motorcycle, but I didn't know if I really wanted these things. I would waffle back and forth, trying to make the perfect choice of pictures. I looked through newspapers and magazines that were lying around the house, but nothing caught my eye. Consequently, I did nothing.

Perfection will do that. If you wait until everything is perfect to act, often nothing happens and your results are zero.

After working months with *Recharge* and increasing my awareness, I realized that it wasn't the pictures that were the problem, it was the fact that I didn't know what I really wanted. I realized that when I chose a picture of something, my paradigm turned on this little voice in my head that said, "You can't get that; quit fooling yourself. You don't really want that. Who do you think you are?"

I stopped looking for pictures. I sat down with a paper and pen and started to answer the question from Chapter One, "What do I really want?" From there, I made a list of pictures I wanted to mount on my vision board. Now that I knew exactly what I wanted, I picked pictures that best represented, and reminded me of, what I really wanted. I googled many of the pictures I wanted online and found them under free picture websites.

The first key to a successful vision board is that it stimulates your thoughts of what you want. You visualize having or being in that place, having that experience, feeling the emotion of that moment.

The second key is to use your vision board every day. If you hang it on the wall, it won't be long before you will walk by it and not remember it is there. Take five minutes every day to stop and look at it with a conscious mind, reviewing and visualizing what you want. Keep it top-of-mind. Update it regularly.

The Last Door

I like to use a door as a metaphor as it has so many parallels to life.

A door, like life, can have several states, and if we are aware of what state the door is in, we can use it to our advantage rather than the door being an obstacle on the pathway of our journey. The door can be open to new adventures, or the door can be closed to new ideas.

Sometimes we take the meaning of a door literally, when the state of the door could be the state of our mindset, opened or closed. What may be an open door of opportunity for one person may be a door of pain and discomfort for another.

I remember the lesson that I learned when Monty, our small Shih Tzu puppy, took on the patio door. Monty was a high-strung puppy that loved to run and play. He chased balls and loved chewing on everything. He was totally house-trained and when he needed to go out, we would open the sliding glass door in the dining room and he would dash full speed out the door onto the patio and into the backyard.

I am not sure what was different on this particular day. It may have been a time when we had just cleaned the glass on the patio door. Monty came running into the dining room and headed to the sliding glass door to run outside. I think he thought the door was open because he ran full speed, smack, into the glass door. It hurt, as we heard a yelp and a scurry through the house. It was a moment of mixed emotions as it was obvious he was hurt, but maybe a little embarrassed at the same time. Realizing what had happened, I called him into the dining room to let him out the sliding door and into the backyard.

Monty approached the open door, stopped and looked up at me as if to say, "You can't fool me twice, open the door." I encouraged him to proceed through the open door, but he wouldn't. Finally, I walked through the door and onto the patio. I stopped and looked back. Monty cautiously took one step forward through the open door, then another, then slowly onto the patio. When he was on the patio he took off, full speed out onto the lawn.

I saw myself in Monty's behaviour. Sometimes we see an opportunity, an investment, a career move, an open door that looks really good and so we take it, only to find out it was not what we expected. Like Monty, we thought the door was open and it was clear sailing, but it wasn't, and we ran full speed into trouble, risk, disappointment, like the closed glass door.

And, like Monty, the next time we hesitate, we doubt, we don't trust the next door to be the opportunity it appears to be. This is very common and we end up not moving ahead, not growing because of one bad experience. Fear and doubt take over our mindset.

We need to *Recharge*, think it through. You are not holding onto the information but to the emotional feeling you had of disappointment when you failed. If you review the facts, most doors are good doors. Once Monty saw me go through the open door, he was willing to try it again. Sometimes we too need encouragement and coaching to once again step forward through the next door of opportunity.

Never look at your next door as your last door, as opportunities are around you constantly.

Recharge Your Door

As we *Recharge*, grow and take on new opportunities, sometimes life doesn't go exactly the way we want or expect it to go, and we need to re-evaluate the door we have chosen to pursue.

Where are you today, right now? Are you trying to *Recharge* something that is not working? Are you stuck, frustrated with the progress you are making? You think you are doing all the right things, and you are still not making the progress you want.

In acknowledging that life cycles, it is also common to experience a time of doubt. A time when you question the decisions you have made. A time when you feel like maybe you picked the wrong door.

If this is you, then let's look at the basics.

Take a reaffirming survey and ask yourself these questions:

1. Do I have a crystal-clear vision of what I want?
2. Do I start my day with the hour of power?
3. Do I think about what I want several times during the day?
4. Do I study every day to learn more to become an expert in my field?
5. Do I have excuses for my environment and my lack of success?
6. Do I learn from my failures or do they hold me back?
7. Do I say I can't do it or do I say how can it be done?
8. Do I take the actions daily that I need to take to reach my goal?

Take time to review these questions and answer them honestly with an open mind. This is a good exercise to do with the assistance of a mentor, someone to walk you through the questions and keep you accountable to answering each one. These questions will help stimulate your thinking and pull you back on track.

In Chapter Four we looked at the Box; what's in your Box and how it got there. When we look at different doors that are presented to us, it is important to keep in mind that we are viewing these doors through the paradigm created by this Box we have.

Many people struggle with financing and the managing of their money. When you ask them if they think the problem is that they never have enough money, they inevitable say the problem is they don't earn enough. This is their paradigm speaking. The real problem is they spend more than they make. If they earn more, they will spend more, and consequently always be broke.

It is important to be aware of your filters and to acknowledge that your resistive feelings, your fears, your doubts and behaviours are a result of the information you are holding in your Box. To change and shift that paradigm requires a change in thinking and mindset. A willingness to consider new ideas.

Discovery Questions:

1/ What event in your life changed the way you think or view something? What shifted your paradigm?

____

____

____

____

____

____

2/ Do you have a vision board? Is it time to create one or update your vision board in light of your new awareness? What would be on it?

____

____

____

____

____

____

Chapter Twelve

Elevate then Celebrate

The Reality of Recharge

I promised you that in this book, *It's time to Recharge*, I would elevate your mindset and increase your sales and business opportunities. I hope you see now, how this can happen. I encourage you to go back and re-read this book over and over, and ponder the questions I have left with you after each chapter. If I can encourage you to keep thinking elevated thoughts, then I have succeeded and I feel fulfilled.

It saddens me to realize that not everyone is ready to open the door to *Recharge*. Not everyone that reads this book will buy into what I am selling. I accept that and acknowledge this is the way life works.

When I stand on stage before an audience of hundreds or thousands of people and share the excitement and benefits of *Recharge,* and how it will change their business and even change their life, I am overwhelmed. I know in my heart that not everyone will go home excited, or be willing to make the changes they need to make. In fact, there may be only a small percentage of people who I have touched and made a positive impact on. It's those that inspire me to continue spreading the message of *Recharge*.

If I keep showing up, and you keep showing up, then someday the timing will be right, the stars will be aligned, our vibration will be in harmony, and you will embrace *Recharge* and know that a recharged mindset is what you need to bridge the gap to what you really want.

What if tomorrow I woke up and everyone was recharged? What if everyone was thinking and functioning at a higher, more productive level? Wouldn't that be awesome?! It may not happen overnight but it can happen, one person at a time.

You must always be aware that people are watching you all the time. Others observe what you do, how you do things, what you say, and how you treat people. I say this because I do it. I observe how others behave, what they do and how they treat people. As you increase your awareness of others, you will be able to connect with others of similar mindsets.

The reality is that you won't connect with everyone equally. I remember, back a few years, attending a local service club meeting as a guest. I had heard what great things they were doing for the community and I thought maybe it was a group I should join and be an active member of. I was new in the area and this would be a way I could meet others in the community and get involved.

I attended one meeting and within an hour of being there, I knew it wasn't a good fit for me. Let's just say I don't drink enough and sports is not a priority in my life. It wasn't a good fit. Looking back now, attending a second meeting may have changed my attitude towards my first impression, but at the time it felt like a good decision.

The reality of *Recharge* is that not everything will work or be a good fit for you. Just because it works for one person doesn't mean it will work for you. We are all different.

A Recharged mind is an open mind, willing to explore new possibilities and new realities.

The Recharged Leader

My focus in this book has primarily been to Recharge YOU. By raising your mindset to think and function at a higher more positive level you can shift to a new dimension that will open doors, attract better relationships and build you a stronger, more profitable business.

As you develop into this new person your courage and confidence will increase dramatically. Your awareness of who you are, and what you have to offer others, will surface in your day-to-day activities. Your personal growth will be like that of an Olympic athlete, practising every day for that big event. You will start to initiate opportunities through inspired creativity. All this, because you made a decision to *Recharge*.

You may not have started this journey with the intention of being a leader or major influencer in your community; however, you have become one by default.

You are now a *LEADER*!

Being raised in a Mennonite community, I came with a very passive approach to life. I talk about this in Chapter Three, "The Kitchen Table." Being a leader or taking the lead in anything was a real stretch for me as my paradigm didn't contain the attributes, beliefs or habits of a leader. I had a strong tendency to sit back and observe, reluctant to get involved. I would participate, but seldom step forward to volunteer.

I have to think I lacked the courage and confidence to step forward and take charge. There was an uncertainty of not knowing, and a fear of making a mistake and being ridiculed. Looking back, I can see I didn't know who I was, what strengths

I had or even what I really wanted in life. Fear and doubt were solidly imbedded in my mindset. They created internal, negative affirmations, and my low self-esteem.

As a Recharged person you will now have an awareness of who you are, what strengths you have, and what you really want in life. Your energy and enthusiasm for life will make you visible, and expose you to opportunities to step up and lead. Others around you will see the courage and confidence you display, and will take your lead as their new direction. Your leadership will lift many of those around you to a higher, more positive level of thinking.

Your decision to step forward may take some effort, and the first time you intentionally do it you will have doubts. Do it anyway. You have what it takes. Don't look for everything to be perfect, as the perfection will come with time and repetition. This was big for me! Your paradigm, what's in your Box, is different from mine, and so your fears and apprehensions will be different as well. No one is born a leader, but we all have different gifts and therefore leading may come easier for some than for others.

Remember the qualities of being Recharged. The higher mindset comes with a healthy, happier attitude. As a leader you want to be strong and assertive without being arrogant and condescending. You lift those around you through gratitude and praise, moulding and developing other leaders along the way.

You have become a Recharged leader by default. It is a position that you will want to treasure because with it comes great responsibility and influence to those around you.

Are you ready to take on the responsibilities of the Recharged leader?

The Four A's of Recharge

When I speak about Recharge to a group, in a workshop, or to an audience, I like to talk about the four pillars that encapsulate, in simplest terms, the essences of what the Recharge process is all about. If you remember these four A's it will help you and remind you to *Recharge*. It will remind you of what step you are at and where your mindset is in the moment.

The four A's of Recharge are: Acknowledge, Awareness, Action, and Accountability.

Acknowledge - The first pillar to *Recharge*, and to raising your mindset to a higher level, is to acknowledge that life cycles. In Chapter Two I talked about the laws that are constant, and that govern the universe. Acknowledging them gives you a consistent base to start from. Know that for every up there is a down, and for every negative there is a positive. We as people are all different and unique. We all have strengths and weaknesses. I acknowledge who I am and what is in my Box.

Awareness - The second pillar to *Recharge,* and to making a conscious decision to think and function at a higher level, is to have awareness, to be consciously aware of what's around you, and the environment in which you live and function, and the circumstances you deal with on a daily basis. Having self-awareness and knowing where you are in life, physically, mentally, spiritually, emotionally, and economically is essential to *Recharge*. Awareness allows you to take responsibility for yourself and where you are right now. Taking responsibility gives you control, to make the changes you need to make, to get you the things you really want, or move you towards becoming the person you really want to become.

Action - The third pillar to *Recharge,* and to becoming the person you really want to become, is Action. You begin with what you want through the creation of your dreams and a vision. From that visualization, you set your goals and develop your emotional excitement towards what your want. This inspires you to take the actions you need to take. First there are the actions and habits you must develop in order to continue being that Recharged person. You must also have a daily routine to create a powerful, positive, affirming mindset. Second, there are the actions you need to take to do the work. Whatever that is in your field of expertise. Gather the knowledge and develop the skills you need to get you the things you really want, or move you towards becoming the person you want to become.

Accountability - The fourth pillar to *Recharge* is Accountability. By keeping you on track, and your momentum strong, you can make sure you are becoming the person you really want to be. Accountability is about reviewing your goals and measuring your results. This is how you can see if you are on track. This is how you can gauge whether or not what you are doing is working, or if you need to make adjustments. You take time to analyze your process, and the actions you took, to see if they are consistent with the results you are looking to achieve. I don't believe we are on this earth to do life all by ourselves. We consult with mentors and coaches to ensure our paradigm is not hindering our progress, or the growth needed to excel to the next level. From accountability we get the feedback we need to make corrections and stay on course.

These are the four pillars, the four A's to *Recharge,* which I encourage you to memorize. They will set you straight when you feel you are off course, struggling to make the progress you want, short of reaching your goals. As you mature in the process you will find that time is not always in your control. The universe is not always attuned to our impatience and urgency. Be consistent, be persistent, but also patient in your pursuit.

Celebrate Your Recharge

As I sit in my office in front of my computer, contemplating my final thoughts to you, I see my red balloon hovering in the space to my right, tethered to a red ribbon holding it from aimlessly floating across the room. It reminds me to celebrate.

In this moment I remind you to celebrate all the time. It is important to be grateful every day. To have a heart of gratitude, not just for others around you but for your divine creator, your God, your higher power that gives you hope, faith and wisdom.

Your Recharged mindset will always look for the good in everything you see. In times of worry, struggle or a catastrophic disaster, seek out the good and seek what you can be grateful for. When you look closely, with a clear mind, you will find the good in everything.

Always look at the glass as half full, rather than half empty.

Look for the lessons that can be learned, the knowledge that can be gathered, the peace that can be found in every event. This is not always easy or immediate. As you are caught up in the moment and overtaken by the emotion of a negative moment, the good may not be obvious or detectable.

Be patient with yourself, seek to be calm through thoughts of gratitude and tranquility. Find peace through controlled thinking, breathing, meditation or prayer. Focus on the joy in your life. Look at the beauty that surrounds you.

It is spring and, in this early morning hour, I hear the birds singing even before the sun appears on the horizon.

It takes practise to be able to celebrate regularly. Like anything we do in life, we must first be consciously aware of what we want, and the thoughts we are thinking in the moment. It takes practise to look for the good, to be optimistic and strive for a continual positive mindset. Refer back to Chapter Two on

"The Elevated Mindset" to refresh your memory.

There will be times when you don't feel like celebrating. Remind yourself that life cycles, and this is normal. Focus on the future, not the past. Your vision of the future is where you want to go. We are moving forward, not backward. If you keep looking back, it will paralyze your thinking and keep you stuck where you are. The past is done. Learn from it and start looking forward.

This switch takes conscious thought in the moment. The conscious thought in the now brings immediate self-awareness. In that moment you can celebrate as you recall your vision for the future.

Celebrating is always more fun when you have someone to celebrate with. As I speak to groups around the world, and share my message of *Recharge*, it is my intention to build a community of like-minded people who network together on an ongoing basis. A network of like-minded people with a passion for positivity who will embrace *Recharge* together.

Would this be a group that you would celebrate with? Visit: www.itstimetorecharge.com

How Do You Want to Finish?

We all have a limited time on this earth. Some of us have more time than others, but none of us has infinite years to live. As I enter the senior years of my life, perhaps the final one third, this becomes more prevalent to me. I have been more aware of people around me passing away. Most of them are older than me but some are younger.

Just this week one of my favourite uncles, Uncle Fred, died. He was 93 years old. He lived a good life, and raised five children. Take a moment and think about someone you lost lately. Someone you may have thought had so much to live for.

Someone whose work wasn't finished here on earth, and was too young to die. We all know people who fit in this category.

Recharge is about living, not dying, but I want to remind you that the clock is ticking. For some of us time is running out. Develop a sense of urgency. Make sure you are doing what is important to you. Make sure each day that you are working towards what you really want to be. Make life a priority. Make living a daily event, with passion and intention.

It is my hope that you are now entering a new chapter of your life, that you are seeking answers to the questions that keep you up at night, and that it is more than curiosity; it is rather a burning desire to find that one thing that will define your purpose in life. Clarify your reason for living on this earth.

Begin each day with joy and gratitude. Do something fun each day, as you never know when it will be your final day. End each day with joy, gratitude and a sense of peace. Trust yourself and have a knowing that you are living the life you are meant to live, and that your quest for purpose is being fulfilled.

You have unlimited potential, and you can achieve anything you can imagine.

And now you have a choice to make. You can stay where you are and keep doing what you're doing. You can keep hoping for a miracle or you can wake up tomorrow morning with Recharge. Begin your morning at 6am and start with your hour of power. Start your journey toward becoming a new you.

How do you want to finish?

I remember reading in Stephen R. Covey's bestselling book, *The Seven Habits of Highly Effective People*, about beginning with the end in mind. This inspired me to ask myself the question, "How do I want to finish?" What does the end look like? When I am gone, what will people say about me? What will be my legacy? What will be written on my tombstone? Will I have made a difference?

I think about this not to feed my ego, but to ask myself what example I am setting. Am I building leaders who will carry on after I am gone? Who will pick up my cause, my sword and shield, and continue the battle to build better individuals, who in turn will build better communities?

Think about your legacy and how you want to finish. What are your characteristics that people will talk about and praise, today, and after you are gone?

My Final Thoughts

As I sit in my chair with my five-year-old grandson Chase sitting on my knee, I wonder what great adventures he will encounter in his lifetime. What journey he will take, what places he will explore. When I look back over the past sixty years of my life and see the many changes that have happened over time, I am overwhelmed and amazed at what huge advances have been made in science and technology. How cities have grown and the continual expansion of our transportation corridors.

Great things happen in the same space that we find Recharged people. Great buildings are built from blueprints that are designed by creative minds. It started with someone's vision, and they had the courage to share it with other visionaries that said yes to new ideas.

Our world needs Recharged people more than ever before. People of faith collaborating together and creating a community of positive thinkers with good intentions. You can be among a unique group of Recharged thinkers that bring hope. What is hope? It is an optimistic state of mind. Hope is based on the expectation of positive outcomes with respect to events and circumstances in one's life. Having hope is having that higher mindset of *Recharge*.

I created *Recharge* to bridge the gap between where you are today and where you dream of being in the future. I have just scraped the surface of *Recharge*. There are many areas I could expand on, dive deeper into and unpack further. This is just the beginning; however, I hope I have given you enough to cause you to be hungry for more, and to use some of the thoughts and ideas I have touched on in this book.

And now, I release you back to the universe of life. You are not the same person as you were when you first picked up this book and started reading. I have put something into your Box, be it ever so small. I have shifted your paradigm, and now it is up to you to decide if you will take action. You are not alone. It's time to Recharge.

Your day has arrived. It is opening night at the *theatre of life*. You have the leading role and it is time to walk onto this huge stage of life.

Your heart is racing, your adrenaline is flowing, your energy is exploding and you are pumped. As you stand tall at centre stage, the music starts playing and the curtain slowly rises. You have arrived. The audience rises to their feet, there is thunderous applause with cheers, whistles, and hoots of appreciation and gratitude!

You have arrived!

You are Fully Charged!

Discovery Questions:

1/ Take a moment and write down 5 things you are grateful for. How does this make you feel?

____
____
____
____
____
____

2/ What are your final thoughts? Write out your big takeaway from this book. What change can you make right now to start your journey towards a Recharged life?

____
____
____
____
____
____

3/ Visit: www.itstimetorecharge.com to connect with *The Recharge Group*.

About the Author

Wayne Kuhn was born on a small farm approximately an hour west of Toronto, Ontario in the mid 1950's. He lived there for the first 14 years of his life before moving with his family to Waterloo, Ontario in 1967. Graduating from college with a Certificate in Electronics Communication and Technology, Wayne went on to work at a large electronic goods manufacturer for the next 15 years, as a computer systems programmer and technician.

In 1987, Wayne entered the real estate industry as a licensed sales representative. Having a love for working and serving people, this opportunity was a perfect fit; a dream come true. As a real estate salesperson he had the freedom of time, a friendly product as everyone needed to live somewhere, and the ability to control his level of income and his love for connecting and helping people.

As a real estate Broker for 33 years, Wayne has achieved many sales awards and worked with the best in the industry. He has learned the secrets to what it takes to be a top producing salesperson, and now he is sharing this knowledge around the world.

In 1993, Wayne became a member of Toastmasters International, an organization dedicated to helping people improve their communication and leadership skills. In 2008 he earned a DTM (Distinguished Toastmaster) designation, the highest level that Toastmaster International awards. Having won many speaking completions at various levels, Wayne went on to doing keynotes and seminars, and facilitating workshops on communication and leadership.

Wayne is married to Suzanne, and together they have a blended family of five boys and, at the moment, six beautiful grandchildren.

Wayne gave birth to Recharge following years of studying salespeople, goal setting, mindset, and searching for the answer to "Why do some people excel in life while others just get by?" A student of Bob Proctor and Sandy Gallagher's program, "Thinking into Results" through the Proctor Gallagher Institute, Wayne was faced with the question: "What do you really want?"

Today, as author of *It's Time to Recharge*, Wayne's focus is on helping people answer this question, and spreading the message of Recharge through seminars, workshops and keynote speeches.